TRUE
STORIES
OF
TRANSFORMED
LIVES

TRUE STORIES *of*
TRANSFORMED LIVES

MIKE NAPPA &
DR. NORM WAKEFIELD

TYNDALE HOUSE PUBLISHERS, INC.
WHEATON, ILLINOIS

Visit Tyndale's exciting Web site at www.tyndale.com

True Stories of Transformed Lives is another creative resource from the authors at Nappaland Communications, Inc. To contact the authors, send email to: nappaland@aol.com

The story "Beginners," which appears on page 183 of this book, is excerpted by permission from *Just for a Moment I Saw the Light* by John Duckworth, copyright © 1994 by the author. Published by Victor Books.

Library of Congress Cataloging-in Publication Data

Nappa, Mike, date
   True stories of transformed lives / by Mike Nappa and Norm Wakefield.
       p.   cm.
   Includes bibliographical references and index.
   ISBN 0-8423-5179-5 (hardcover : alk. paper)
   1. Converts—United States Biography.   2. Christian biography—United States.   I. Wakefield, Norm.   II. Title.
BV4930.N36   1999
248.2'4'0922—dc21   99-23255
[B]

Printed in the United States of America

07   06   05   04   03   02   01   00   99
10   9   8   7   6   5   4   3   2   1

For Edith Wakefield,
a woman who has spent her life
giving it away.
M.N. & N.W.

Contents

Acknowledgments

I (Mike) would like to gratefully acknowledge a few important people. First, Meg Diehl was Tyndale's acquisitions editor whose passion for this book overcame my initial decision not to write it. Next, my friend John Duckworth graciously allowed me to include his eloquent retelling of his father's salvation story. When I grow up, I want to be a writer just like John!

Also, I treasure my wife, Amy, who had the privilege of leading our son to Jesus and who grants me the privilege of being her husband. In Amy's eyes I see a reflection of the joy of my salvation, and I am grateful for it.

My father-in-law and coauthor, Dr. Norm Wakefield, willingly shared his wealth of stories and considerable writing talent to make this book a reality. Without him, *True Stories of Transformed Lives* would simply be an idea percolating in my head. He is irreplaceable, both as a coauthor and a friend.

Norm's mother, Edith Wakefield, is the woman to whom this book is dedicated. After seeing Norm's Christian example, Edith gave her heart to Christ during a church service in 1955. She describes the moment this way:

"Every part of the service spoke to me. But the Lord used the music in a special way. It seemed to be calling me to open my heart to Christ. So on that Sunday morning, February 27, 1955, when the pastor extended an invitation to come to the front of the church for counsel, I knew I had to respond.

"A warm, gentle lady took me aside and explained the gospel to me, and I trusted in Jesus' death on Calvary's cross on my behalf. A few minutes later I discovered that my daughter, Jane, had also entered into a relationship with Christ. I was overjoyed."

Though in her mid-eighties, Edith still teaches a women's Sunday school class. Twice a week she drives to a nursing home to cheer her oldest son who lives there. Those who know her admire her fruitful life. Edith's is a wonderful story of salvation and lifelong servanthood. As the Scripture says, her children rise up and call her blessed—though we are surely the blessed ones.

Finally, I acknowledge Jesus Christ, my Lord, my Savior, my highest reason for living. I met him almost two decades ago. Apart from him, I certainly would have nothing to write about. Despite popular opinion, the words of the old hymn are still true:

To the utmost, Jesus saves.

Introduction

The words on the computer screen captured my attention, practically demanding I stop and read. I was logged on to the Internet, scanning through the message boards of Christianity Online and not really searching for anything. I was just passing a few free moments surfing the Net.

Then I saw the posting from a user called StrongWord, and I had to stop. The message said: "Praise God, my 7-year-old son accepted Jesus today! There's a party goin' on in heaven today!"

That was all, but it was enough. I tried to continue my scanning of other messages, but my mind kept straying back to that simple declaration. I wondered what had happened to bring that child into a meeting with God—and I wished I had been there to see it.

Moments later I came across a posting from a woman who called herself GodsHeir. The message read: "I am a 35-year-old prodigal daughter. I was very rebellious as an older teen, had a child out of wedlock at 20, lots of other junk. All the while, my parents (especially my mother) had been praying for me. I finally came home and asked God why did I have to waste so many years in sin and garbage . . ."

At that moment, this woman came face-to-face with the Savior Jesus Christ. Her life has been radically altered. Her message finished with an encouragement for those who have a loved one gone astray. It was signed, "A former stray sheep brought back to the sheepfold by the Master."

Why did this story touch me? I wondered. *I don't*

even know this woman! So why was I so interested in hearing how she met Christ? Or how that little boy met Christ?

Then I realized something. It's true I don't know GodsHeir or StrongWord's son, but I do know their Savior. Just like he touched them, Jesus Christ reached out to me, using distinct people, places, and life experiences to introduce me to himself.

We three aren't the only ones God has been busy meeting. If the published estimates are correct, there are nearly two billion Christians currently living on planet Earth.[1]

It's curious how long it would take to meet two billion people. Assuming one minute per person, you'd have to spend about 3,805 years just to introduce yourself to each person who claims to have met Jesus!

Yet God has introduced himself to each one, intimately and personally. That makes me wonder: How do people meet God?

Does he come with a bang, exploding into our consciousness and demanding our surrender? Does he arrive quietly, unnoticed until that moment of realization when it becomes clear he's been nearby all along? Does he show himself with startling clarity or with muddy impressions? Does he call from a distance? whisper in our ears? impress us with his power? touch the longing within?

The answer to all these questions, it seems, is yes. People meet God in all these ways—and

[1]*The World Almanac and Book of Facts* 1997 (Mahwah, N.J.: World Almanac Books, 1996).

more. In every instance, they walk away from that meeting changed forever. It's impossible to meet the Holder of eternity and not be changed, either for good or for ill.

In spite of the billions of introductions God has made, we tend to forget those meetings. We lose interest. We lose the moment. We reminisce about weddings, holidays, and vacations, but we neglect to pass on the stories of how we came to faith in Jesus Christ. We smile, nod, and let the memories fade like yesterday. Yet it was in those moments of meeting that we obtained salvation, that God opened the doors of eternity for one more passenger on the journey to heaven. We forget and are the poorer for it.

After that day of Net surfing, I started a little experiment. I started asking Christians to tell me about when they first met God. The stories came reluctantly at first, almost embarrassingly in some instances. But everyone had a story, and every story was different. And when a group got started, sometimes they wouldn't stop!

The stories people told were sometimes brief, sometimes lengthy. Some were dramatic and filled with miracles; others were simple and plain but still life changing. The people who shared their stories gained strength from remembering when and where they met God. When such a memory is shared, others have a chance to respond to the one who loves us into his kingdom. These stories remind us that God hasn't retired but is actively involved in people's lives today.

My experiment is not finished, but I feel selfish

keeping it all to myself. I recruited Dr. Norm Wakefield, a former pastor and keeper of many stories himself, to join with me in writing about these moments of salvation. Together we're happy to pass on the collection to you.

Take a little time to reminisce with us now, to relive divine moments of people just like you. It's our prayer that today—somehow, some way—you too will meet God through the stories in this book.

Mike Nappa, 1998

1

THE VIEW FROM
THE CAR SEAT

The conversation on the set of the TV sitcom *Step by Step* went something like this:

"We've got a problem."

"What is it now?"

"It's Chris. He won't say his lines."

"What do you mean he won't say his lines? He's an actor, isn't he? He's memorized the script, hasn't he? So what's the problem?"

"Well, he says that the lines as written have 'bad words' in them. He says he doesn't feel right saying them."

"Let me talk to him. . . ."

Teen actor Christopher Castile picks up the story there. "I don't use bad language on the show or in real life. They had me saying a few lines I felt uncomfortable with, a few bad words that I didn't feel like saying. I told them, 'You know, listen. I'm real uncomfortable about this thing.'"

The directors were gentle, but firm. "Chris, the lines lose their meaning without it."

Chris didn't want to cause too much of a fuss. *Isn't being an actor on a television sitcom every teenager's dream?* A strong childhood memory anchored him and gave Chris the courage to make his stand against foul language during television acting.

"I was very young, around three years old. I remember we were driving and I was in my car seat. . . ."

Trees whizzed by. Traffic wove in and out. Three-year-old Chris was lost in the world of in-between, waiting to arrive at the chosen destination. Something outside his mother's car captured his imagination and attention. He gazed up intently, watching the clouds shift and billow as they decorated the sky. His heart was piqued with curiosity, so he asked a question.

"Mom, who's God?"

Chris's mother carefully explained to her son who God is, how we can know him, and how we can become his children. By the time Chris's mom had parked the car, Chris had decided to become a child of God.

Chris remembers the decision. "I just asked her a lot of questions, and I was saved right there in the car. Spontaneous!"

A dozen years later, that experience was still vivid and powerful enough to give Chris the courage to risk his reputation as an actor in order to avoid speaking words he knew Jesus thought shameful. "My mom [who is also Chris's manager] and I kept on pushing and pushing. We said,

'We're just not comfortable with this.' It wasn't like a big fight or anything, but they just thought cursing wasn't that big of a deal."

Unexpectedly, a few of the show's writers joined Chris in his objection and deleted the offensive words from the script. As it turned out, a couple of the writers were also Christians. "We know the feeling, Chris," they said, "so we'll just take it out."

Perhaps they, too, had seen the clouds and found for themselves the answer to the question "Who's God?"

FIRST CHURCH OF
MCDONALD'S

Kurt Garland is a skinny guy—but don't be fooled by his trim appearance. He's aggressive on a basketball floor ("The guy's all elbows!" says a friend who guarded Kurt once) and a fount of seemingly endless energy when pounding the drums for his church's worship band.

Kurt's favorite fuel for all that energy is burgers and fries. This guy is hungry all the time. He's always happy to eat your leftovers and has no trouble eating a meal too big for guys twice his size. As a young teacher, he often left a sign in the middle-school cafeteria saying, "Please leave all uneaten sandwiches for Mr. Garland."

"I'd feast on roast-beef day!" says Kurt. "None of those kids liked the sandwiches, so there was always plenty left for me."

With such a healthy appetite, Kurt thought he'd found the perfect job: manager at a local

McDonald's! "Anything left over at the end of the day was fair game. I never went home hungry."

Unfortunately, Kurt also had unhealthy appetites. "I was a pretty hard person," he admits. "Drank a lot. Did drugs." He hungered for something more in life, something deeper. He tried to fill that hunger through partying, but he wasn't satisfied.

That was when he noticed something at work—strange people working with him. He confronted his coworkers. "What makes you so different? You're joyful, you're happy. You don't cuss, you don't drink, you don't really care about peer pressure. Why are you so different?"

These strange people had only one explanation: Jesus. They were Christians, and during shifts at work they befriended Kurt and told him more about Jesus Christ.

Kurt was interested but unwilling to make a change. Still, he found something very attractive about these Christians. They all started spending time together after work, building friendships beyond McDonald's.

One night they were relaxing, hanging out at a friend's house. The conversation turned to Jesus, and eventually one friend asked Kurt if he wanted to become a Christian.

The hunger burned inside Kurt's soul. He desperately wanted what these people had, but he wasn't sure Jesus was truly all they said he was. He mused for a minute. "OK. I'll try Jesus for thirty days and see if it changes me."

Two decades later, Kurt laughs when recalling

the "Jesus trial period." "Obviously, I kept on going. It was a very exciting time for me. It reached a point where I was actually telling customers at McDonald's about Jesus—I almost got fired for it!"

Each day of that thirty-day trial (and each day since it), Kurt found himself irresistibly drawn to the Bible. He read it and asked many questions of his Christian friends. During that time he discovered more about Jesus. Jesus Christ truly was the nourishment his spirit had been craving for so long. "I felt an overwhelming peace during that time. I was loved by God, and it didn't matter what other people thought."

Twenty years later this skinny guy with a giant appetite still remembers how he ate at McDonald's for fuel but found nourishment for his soul in the Bible.

3

CUSTOMERS FROM HEAVEN

"Eddie! You've got a customer!"

Twenty-one-year-old Eddie Elguera sighed
and went to the counter of the fast-food Mexican
restaurant his brother owned. He was happy to
be working and near his family, but these things
reminded him of how far he had fallen.

Five years ago, still in high school, Eddie Elguera
had been the undisputed king of skateboarding in
America. He had invented tricks that soon became
standards in the skateboard community and had
given them wacky names: "the Elguerial,"
"Frontside Rock-n-Roll" and "Fakie Ollie."
Delighted fans called him "El Gato" ("the cat")
because no matter how many times he might fall
off his board, he always landed on his feet.

Eddie's aggressive and innovative style earned
him other honors. *Skateboarder Magazine* named
him their "Skateboarder of the Year." The U.S.

Amateur Skateboard Association named him their national champion. A year later the professional skateboard community named this ingenious teen from Lake Arrowhead, California, the Gold Cup Series winner—making him the number one pro skateboarder in the world.

But while he was at the top professionally, Eddie's personal life was headed toward the bottom. The stress of fame, the glare of the national media's spotlight, and a shower of money from skateboard sponsorships overloaded him. Despite success, Eddie wasn't satisfied. He started looking elsewhere for satisfaction.

"I just started partying," Eddie says. "I thought I was always going to have the money and the vehicles and everything. And basically, within four years, you know, I had lost it—lost it all."

Washed-up at twenty-one, Eddie Elguera found himself working for his brother, serving Mexican fast food to Lake Arrowhead's residents and tourists. That was when sixty-eight-year-old May Hubolt, hankering for a burrito, stepped up to the counter and into Eddie's life.

"Man, she was [a] fireball!" Eddie remembers with a laugh. "I tell you. She was *excited* about the Lord."

May ordered her lunch, then paused to chat. During the course of the conversation, Eddie shared about his rise and fall in the world of pro sports. When he finished, he shrugged. "You know I was just kind of looking . . ." His voice trailed off into silence.

May didn't waste a minute. She drew herself up

and looked him in the eye. "Eddie, what you're looking for, you're not going to find in skateboarding—no matter how good you were—or in drugs and alcohol. What you're looking for is Jesus Christ, a relationship with him." Eddie's mother and brother came out to hear what this old woman was talking about, and she told them the same thing too.

Eddie knew she was right. "She shared the gospel with me and then asked me if I wanted to receive the Lord. So I received the Lord that day." Eddie's mother and brother also became Christians!

A few weeks later, May was back in the restaurant. She'd been visiting churches near where Eddie lived, trying to find a good one for these new Christians to join. She took the family to a church pastored by Jim Cobrae. Eddie (now a youth pastor himself) grins. "And actually, he's still my pastor today."

More than a decade later, Eddie concludes his story this way: "A lot of people think, 'Aww, these old people aren't going to make a difference.' But you know what? May Hubolt *did* make a difference—for me, and for my mother and my brother."

4

THE "LOL" AND
THE BOXER

In 1985 it would have been futile to say to Sue
Sawyer, "You worry about life too much. It has
no meaning. Relax and enjoy it."

Sue couldn't do that. She worked as a nurse in
an intensive care unit at her hospital. Every day she
was confronted with patients who were about to
die. If she wasn't thinking about death, they were.
When her patients weren't thinking about death,
they were reliving their lives and sharing their fears
and feelings with her.

"I felt privileged to be the recipient of their
reflections," Sue says. "I knew that these World
War II and Korean War vets were speaking words
of wisdom. Some men had been at Normandy.
They told of being in foxholes with guns blazing
and bullets flying overhead. Some stories may have
been embellished with time, but I didn't mind.
That just made them more fascinating!"

Her patients often spoke of loved ones—spouses, children, and friends. All of them were teaching Sue how to value people and things. Her patients urged her to lay aside things that weren't that important. So many men and women said, "Don't worry about accumulating *stuff*. It has no meaning now."

Two individuals are etched in Sue's memory. One was a World War II vet. The other was an LOL—an acronym medical people use for an endearing *little old lady*. This LOL was in Sue's unit just a short time.

One day this LOL clicked on her call light, and Sue was the only nurse available to respond. "I went in, even though she was not my patient that day. I so clearly remember entering and asking her what she wanted. 'You're not my patient today. Do you want me to get your nurse?' I asked. I knew how much LOLs like to talk, and that day I was busy."

The lady responded, "I want to tell you something."

Sue protested, "I'm not your nurse. I'll go and get her."

But the lady was insistent. "No need for that. I just wanted to tell *you* something. Now shut the door, honey." Sue knew that she was in for a long talk. *Arrgh,* she thought. *Oh well. I bet the hours pass by too slowly for her. I guess I can listen for a bit. Poor thing.*

The lady took Sue's hand and said, "I know I'm dying. I have waited my whole life to see Jesus, and now I will see him soon. I am so excited." She paused, patted Sue's hand, and then squeezed it. "That's all I want to say, honey."

Sue muttered, "Isn't that wonderful!" and left feeling puzzled and troubled.

Later, Sue witnessed a man's death. He was one of the World War II vets who had been a boxer in the Air Force. "I stood outside his room and watched. As his blood pressure and heart rate began to decelerate, he started wildly swinging his arms in the air. He must have thought he was losing consciousness during a boxing match. The picture spoke loudly; it was *so* symbolic. I stood transfixed, watching. The man was raging against the 'dying of the light.' He was so different from the lady I had talked to the previous week."

Sue went home that night deeply troubled by the boxer's death. *He was so different from the little lady. I wonder which way I will face death—at peace, the way the little old lady did, or swinging wildly, fighting against the unknown, the way the boxer did.*

Sue's heart had been well prepared by the two events with patients. A few days later her friend Diane invited her to a spaghetti dinner. As they chatted, the matter of Sue's relationship to Jesus Christ arose. Diane told her of a heavenly Father's desire for her to spend eternity with him. That night Sue committed her life to Jesus, asking him to forgive her sins and to prepare a place in heaven for her.

"What a creative God. He orchestrated my circumstances so perfectly that they collectively wooed me to him. I'm touched by the fact that he knew how to gently call me, a sinner, to come home."

5

SAME OLD ROUTINE?

Eleven-year-old Priscilla knew the Sunday church routine by heart. Go to church. Sit on the side of the auditorium with the other kids. Sing. Listen to Reverend Stacks preach. Go up to the altar to sing and pray. Go home for supper with the family— Mom, Dad, her seven older brothers and two younger sisters.

This bright Sunday in 1975 started out no differently from any other. One by one the family members filed into the church, prepared for the morning service. The music was always Priscilla's favorite, and she sang enthusiastically! Her whole family contributed to the service by singing and clapping, waving tambourines, and breaking into impromptu harmonies. The family served God with their musical talents. Priscilla loved being at church with her family and friends.

Reverend Stacks finally got up to preach the sermon. He was a dedicated man of God and a wise loving pastor, but he could not hold the attention of eleven-year-old Priscilla. Priscilla tried to listen, but occasionally her mind wandered away from Reverend Stacks's words.

Then came the time for more music. Priscilla readily joined the others in singing and marched her way down to the altar for the service finale. It was there that the unexpected happened.

Unheard by the rest of the folks gathered in the church, the Spirit of God was speaking to young Priscilla. Midway through a song, she leaned back and for the first time considered what she was doing when she sang praises to God.

"I sat back and just really thought about the goodness of the Lord," she says now, "how good he had been to me up until that point. I decided I wanted to live my life for him because *I wanted* to live my life for him."

No longer would church be just a family routine. No longer would songs of praise simply be words and tunes that someone else taught her. Kneeling at the altar that day, Priscilla had gone beyond singing and had entered into a relationship with Jesus Christ.

More than twenty years later, Priscilla continues to sing, going by the childhood name her family gave her: CeCe. A professional musician who has won many Grammy and Dove awards, CeCe Winans is one of Christian music's most respected performers. Unlike some of her contemporaries, she remains committed to creating music that plainly praises her Savior. Back in 1975 God met Priscilla and transformed her church routine into a sincere, praise-filled heart habit.

6

SUNDAY MORNING AT
THE SHAVING MIRROR

Unwashed and unkempt, Ken Wakefield stood in front of the shaving mirror. It was Sunday, and though he hadn't been there for some time, Ken felt that today would be a good day to visit church.

Ken had had a difficult upbringing. When he was a child, his mother had already been a victim of verbal spousal abuse for many years. "I can't take any more of this," Ken's mother said when he was fourteen. During the summer of 1947, she took Ken's younger brother and sister and fled the family and farm that were her home. Ken was left behind—but not for long. About one month later Ken and his older brother slipped away from the farm and were reunited with their mother at a relative's home.

During that brief stay at his aunt and uncle's house he first heard bits and pieces of the good news about Jesus Christ. Ken's uncle and aunt attended a Wesleyan Methodist church in the small community of Buena Vista, New York. Ken remembers the preacher talking about a person being "saved," but he was confused by the word. What in the world did it mean to be "saved"? Too shy to ask for more information, Ken left the church with unanswered questions.

He then moved to the country to live with his grandfather and grandmother. Being a strong fourteen-year-old, he loved to work in the fields with his granddad. One night after a hard day's work he was stretched out on his bed listening to the radio: WWVA in Wheeling, West Virginia. That night he heard a country preacher speak about Jesus Christ and his death on the cross on our behalf.

"All you need to do is ask Jesus into your heart, and you'll go to heaven," the preacher said. Ken recalls now, "I really wanted that, so I asked Jesus to forgive my sins and let me go to heaven some-day. But I still didn't really understand what it meant and didn't know anyone I could talk to about it, so I put it aside and soon forgot about it."

The transition to adulthood was not easy for Ken. He soon discovered alcohol, seemingly an instant cure for his insecurities. A couple of drinks chased away his shyness, making him feel ready to tackle anything.

What Ken didn't realize was that one day he'd have to tackle an addiction to alcohol. By the time he recognized the danger, Ken was trapped—a slave to the addicting power of drink. It dictated what he thought about, where he went, with whom he associated, and how he behaved. He finally had to speak the horrifying words, "I am an alcoholic."

Ken knew he was in trouble. "All I could picture was that I was on a very high slide, going down real fast, and soon I would hit bottom and be in hell."

By now Ken was married with a house full of children. But Ken's wife was ill in the hospital. Coming home from visiting his wife, Ken was so depressed that he contemplated suicide. It seemed the only realistic solution.

Sitting on the couch with his head in his hands, Ken felt he'd hit the bottom of the slide. His life couldn't get any worse than this. It was there that God chose to meet Ken Wakefield. Suddenly, unexpectedly, Ken had a distinct sense of the Lord speaking to him. The words he heard were, "Ken, if you do what I ask, I'll get you out of this mess."

Ken was both scared and excited. His immediate reaction was to call on his Christian neighbors, Vi and Ab, and tell them what had happened. This godly couple stopped what they were doing and explained to Ken who Jesus is and the good news about sin and forgiveness. They prayed with him, and he went home.

Ken was actually a little disappointed. Nothing happened, it seemed—no skyrockets, no lightning flashing, no earth trembling. Ken felt almost the same as before. Shrugging his shoulders, he went to bed.

The next morning Ken got up to go to church. "When I got up, I decided to visit Vi and Ab's church. I went into the bathroom to shave. When I looked in the mirror I realized that this was the first morning I could remember when I didn't have to have a drink. I started to feel a warmth that began at my feet and rose slowly to the top of my head. I felt as though I was being unzipped from head to toe and someone was hosing me out with a big hose! I felt clean! (And I still have the feeling.)"

The oppressive weight of guilt that Ken had carried for so long fell off his back. A profound sense of freedom swept over him. It was then that he knew Jesus had "saved" him and changed him forever. "From that day on, a glass of beer had the same appeal to me as a glass of motor oil!"

7

THREE CHEERS
FOR GOD

A cheerleader since the eighth grade, Cindy Pilger was certain she would join the varsity squad and cheer her team from the sidelines throughout her high school days. But this year when the tryouts were held, Cindy was not chosen.

Cindy was devastated. She had already blocked out time during the summer to attend the varsity cheerleaders' camp, and her parents had already scrimped together enough money for her to go. Now another girl would take her place at that camp.

It seemed a waste to sit at home when she had the time and money to go to camp, so Cindy decided she'd go to another camp that year—something called "Young Life Camp." This other, "religious" camp turned out to be an exhilarating experience. The entire staff enthusiastically greeted the campers. Cindy's counselor was a sincere loving person. The physical environment, the sensitive staff, and the good-natured laughter softened her heart. *This is like heaven,* she thought, beginning to feel healed from the tryout disappointment.

Cindy had always felt at home around Christians. She'd heard the gospel many times in her church, but it had never felt personal to her. Every day during camp she heard about Christ's love in a new way. She found her heart responding in deeper ways than she had thought possible. In spite of the recent disappointment she began to grasp the depth of God's love for her. She began to believe that she could trust him with her future.

On the last day campers were challenged to sit alone and make some decisions about what the Lord had revealed to them. Cindy walked into the forest and plopped down at the foot of a tree. In the solitude she encountered the Lord of the universe in a way she'd never known. In a deep, personal, and real way, Cindy opened her heart to Jesus.

She prayed, "Lord, I know that you're real. I believe that you have good things planned for my life. I want to know you." Then in the stillness of the woods, a peace and joy swept over her and settled into her heart. A hope welled up, assuring her that her newfound Lord had a bright future for her.

Everyone gathered back together, and a camp leader said, "If you've committed your life to Christ, stand up." Cindy felt awkward at first because she didn't want others to realize that she had never known Christ in a personal way. But with shaking knees she stood with the rest. Celebration over the new Christians burst forth as campers, counselors, and staff wept with joy for their friends. Many people hugged each other.

When Cindy returned home, she knew that she had met God at camp. She knew that he had changed her forever. A hunger to know him caused her to begin to read her Bible in a new way. She couldn't believe how the words took on new meaning. Often they seemed written just for her.

She also began to tell her younger sister, Stacey, of this newfound Friend. They had always been close, so it was natural for her to open her heart and share this priceless gift. In time Stacey, too, came to entrust her life to Jesus Christ.

All this happened that summer in 1970. Nearly three decades later, Cindy Pilger Martin still finds strength in what her Lord taught her about joy coming out of disappointment.

8

IN THE LINE
OF FIRE

After spending over ten years working as a news correspondent for CBS radio in Jerusalem, Israel, David Dolan has seen many things. He has witnessed numerous conflicts in the Middle East, given firsthand reports on terrorist activities, broadcast news from Jerusalem while Saddam Hussein's SCUD missiles rained down on the city (during the Gulf War), seen a rocket explode fifty feet from him while standing on a friend's doorstep, and been a spectator for air battles between Israeli and Syrian jet fighters. One such dogfight ended with the tail of a Syrian plane crashing a few hundred yards behind his office.

So what keeps this guy from Idaho reporting news from the heart of Israel? It started back in 1973.

As a teenager who'd been raised in a strongly Catholic home, David rejected his family's beliefs and announced he was an agnostic. "Didn't go over real well with my folks or extended family!"

During this time David experimented with substance abuse and began working at a nearby restaurant. The cook at the restaurant was heavily into the occult and had spent time with Charles Manson. She struck up a friendship with David and other young people in the area.

"My girlfriend and I and others would go over to her home and spend a lot of time there having marijuana parties." It was there he was introduced to the world of dark spirituality.

Then, unexpectedly, one of David's older brothers became a Christian. "He shared the gospel with me, and I rejected it." Even though David rejected Christ, his brother's example sparked an interest in the Bible. That Christmas, David's brother gave him a Bible and a book on Israel's place in Bible prophecy. David refused to read them.

Then just after the new year, David came face-to-face with the dangers of dabbling in the occult. "I actually had a demon appear to me and offer to give me power if I would worship it. I was quite shaken by the experience because I was just starting to really accept that there might indeed be a spirit world. I actually turned on and off lights and tried to make the thing go away and pretend it was just an illusion, but I knew that it was real. It was frightening, and I was freaked! The first thing I did was put on my shoes . . . [then] went for a walk and got out of there. I was hoping that when I came back it would be gone, but it was still there."

David told the cook at the restaurant about the demon visitor. She came over, saw it, and confirmed that it was a dark spirit. She was unfazed by it, but for David, it meant a turning to God.

"Thank God I did reject it," he says now. "And that night I picked up the Bible—started reading it."

The Spirit of God softened this self-proclaimed agnostic, and David finally asked Jesus to forgive and save him. He became a Christian, turning his back completely on the occult and agnosticism and vowing to follow Christ anywhere.

David also began reading the Bible prophecy book his brother had given him, a book by Hal Lindsay. "Immediately my heart was turned toward Israel. Immediately I determined that I would go there someday."

After that, David immersed himself in the Bible, studying about—and growing to love—Israel. In 1980 he was able to visit Israel as an exchange student. He liked Israel so much that he stayed there, returning to the U.S. only for vacations and to visit family. By 1988 he had started his career as a CBS news correspondent in Jerusalem, and that's where David Dolan still lives.

9

FROM SILVER SPOON TO
GOLDEN GOSPEL

Diane Larson had everything going for her. "I was
born with a silver spoon in my mouth. I was
indulged, affirmed, and eulogized by two loving
parents." As she grew to adulthood she achieved
academic excellence, athletic prowess, and
distinction in leadership. Her family trained her
religiously; they were committed to participate in
the programs of the local Presbyterian church. If
anyone had a promising future, it was Diane.

In the spring of 1984 Diane found herself far
from her dreams. Picture the scenes of Diane's life
now. . . . Diane's loving parents are separated. Her
own marriage has dissolved. She's living wildly with
a passionate, athletic "Don Juan" who will end up
in prison. Life is one extravagant indulgence after
another: sports, parties, drugs, and travel.

What Diane doesn't realize is that her world is
in the process of disintegrating. Her relationship

with "Don Juan" is extremely volatile and destructive. More and more she recognizes the vacuum in her soul. She realizes that her upright family was trying to help her, but all she sees now is the emptiness in her soul.

Life is coming apart at the seams. And at the point of the unraveling, God steps in.

"Come with me to my church," a voice says. It's Kristi, Diane's friend. "I think you'll like it."

Diane has it all—but she knows she's still missing something. She knows she needs strength greater than her own. "OK, I'll go."

Sitting inconspicuously in the morning worship service, Diane listened intently as a soloist named Ellie performed a song. Diane remembers now, "I felt like an arrow pierced my heart. I was humbled and broken in spirit. I left the church that morning deeply troubled."

After church Kristi invited Diane to her home for lunch. That afternoon she told Diane about the grace that Jesus provides and about the promise of new life and forgiveness that comes with giving your heart to Christ. Diane knew she needed that grace; she craved that new life and longed for that forgiveness.

Diane prayed right there in Kristi's home and asked for God's grace in Christ. That day the silver spoon was replaced with the golden love of the gospel.

10

A REASON TO
BE SCARED?

Seventeen-year-old Elijah Stone was scared, but it wasn't the same as before. As a younger teen growing up in a single-parent family, he had nurtured a habit of substance abuse—drinking to excess and using drugs to fill his time. Then he overdosed.

Alone through that turbulent night, Eli screamed for help, praying all night that God would rescue him from his self-inflicted torture. He made it through and, by the time he was fifteen, had finally kicked the drug habit for good. But the scars of that experience remained.

When he found himself homeless as a high schooler, he worried about how he was going to eat, where he was going to sleep, and how he could avoid being mugged. Those were good reasons to feel afraid.

After Elijah's parents split up, his mother said he

was too much to handle and sent him off to live with his dad. His dad, a Vietnam veteran and a veteran of gang activity, was angry. Elijah never knew exactly what his dad would do when angry. But Dad was different now—said he was a Christian, that Jesus changed his life. Instead of hatred and anger, now Dad exhibited calmness, love. He had a much gentler attitude, and he smiled more—something Elijah wasn't used to.

That's why Eli was scared. Dad sat right next to him in the pew, and Dad was the one who had brought Eli with him to church. It was weird to see him so in love with God. Something caused Eli's heart to beat fast, making him short of breath. That church service in Thousand Oaks, California, alarmed him.

"It is by grace you have been saved," quoted the speaker to the congregation, to Eli. That Scripture from Ephesians 2:8 (NIV) was the source of Eli's apprehension. He felt shocked and drawn to grace—unconditional, undeserved grace offered by God.

Is there grace for me? Eli wondered to himself. *A rebel, a heartbreak to my parents, a homeless kid, a drug abuser?*

Then finally, slowly, the realization dawned on Eli. *God . . . loves . . . ME!* He realized what had frightened him. He was scared of hope, scared to believe that this love he so desperately wanted could actually be true. What if this all turned out to be a sham, a false promise of love? Then again, what if it were true?

For once in his life, Eli wanted something more

than he wanted drugs, more than he wanted his parents to reconcile, more than anything. Eli wanted to run to the Person who loved him in spite of what he had done, in spite of who he had become. Elijah Stone wanted to run to Jesus.

The pastor moved toward the close of the service, offering anyone the opportunity to come down to the altar and pray to receive Jesus Christ's love and forgiveness. The pastor counted to three, indicating that all who wanted to receive Jesus should stand at that point. Eli's knees felt weak; his heart pounded. But he stood, straight and tall. Minutes later down at the altar, Eli asked Jesus to save and forgive him. Eli accepted God's love and grace. And then he was no longer afraid.

Three years later, Eli taught himself to play guitar. Seven years after that, he released his first Christian album on the ForeFront Records label beside artists dc Talk and Rebecca St. James. Now an adult, Eli sings about the difference Christ can make in a person's life, especially to one who has doubted it.

"God loved me first. God loves me no matter what. It broke my heart, man! Like, if that's who you are, Jesus, I'll love you for the rest of my life. Who can turn that away? It was love that I didn't have to earn. It's still what I rely on today."

11

AN ORPHAN FINDS
A HOME

It's painful when a mom and dad want to split up
and go their own way. But it's even more painful
when both parents say, "We don't want to be
bothered with you kids. We don't want you!"

Gary Dodd heard that message from his parents
when he was eight years old. Gary and his four-
year-old brother were abandoned, left to be cared
for by their grandmother. Gary's grandmother soon
found a children's home in their home state of
California and placed the boys there. Now they
were truly orphans.

Adelide Christian Home for Children was
located in southern California and operated by
Dick and Mary Matthews. The Matthewses were
kind and loving Christians who endeavored to
create a place that would live up to its name:
home. To Gary, they succeeded.

"I found at the home a love and stability I'd not known before." He also found something more.

One Sunday evening the Matthewses and their wards returned from a worship meeting at the LaBrea Gospel Chapel. As Dick recalled the event he said, "In my view the sermon that night left much to be desired. The speaker was a good man, but a preacher he was not! We came home tired [and] discouraged and got the children to bed."

With the children in bed, Dick and Mary retired to the kitchen to sip a Pepsi and plan the week's menus. In the stillness they heard the squeak of a door and the quiet voice of Gary Dodd. He was calling for Mr. Matthews. Dick was annoyed at the interruption. "What do you want?"

"Mr. Matthews," came the reply, "would you please come and tell me how to be saved?" Dick immediately regretted his irritation. Finding his Bible, he shared with young Gary the story of how Jesus had come to earth, died for our sins, and then risen back to life. He told Gary that he, too, could pray and accept Jesus' gift of forgiveness and life. Right there, among half-drunk Pepsi cans and unfinished menus, Gary received that gift.

With tears in his eyes, Gary approached Mrs. Matthews. "Mrs. Matthews, I just accepted Jesus as my Savior." She threw her arms around Gary and hugged him joyfully.

When Gary spoke of this event later, he marveled at the way the Lord weaves people into our lives. "The preacher, Charlie Wilson, talked about knowing where one would go in the hereafter, sort of a 'hell-fire' message. But what touched me—an abandoned child—was knowing that those who loved me were going to heaven. I knew the Matthewses were going to be with Jesus, and I wanted to be there with them. So I wanted Jesus as my Savior too."

Dick Matthews agreed. "It was one of those memorable moments when we learned this Scripture in a new way: 'The joy of the Lord is your strength.' Suddenly we had physical energy to go on, and spiritually we were flying."

Our Lord had not only met Gary Dodd but encouraged two servants who needed refreshment.

12

MISS RUTH, THE CANDY LADY

I wonder who is singing in that house, Gene Ratley thought as he walked past a home noisy with music. *Maybe some of the neighborhood kids can tell me.*

When he asked a friend later, the pal responded, "Oh that's Miss Ruth, the Candy Lady. She has a candy store in the front of her house! Every Wednesday afternoon she has a Bible class down in her basement. We sing songs and hear Bible stories. Afterwards she gives us cookies, and sometimes we even get some candy."

The thought of free cookies and candy motivated this eleven-year-old boy to attend. He was looking for some fun, and free candy might help. Adjusting to the move from North Carolina to this rough neighborhood in Baltimore hadn't been easy for Gene. His dad left the family when Gene was three, and his mom worked hard each day to provide for the family. Perhaps Miss Ruth's Bible class would fill some of Gene's free time and would be a fun place to go.

The next Wednesday, as soon as the three o'clock bell rang at school, Gene practically ran to Miss Ruth's house. He found her to be a gentle woman in her seventies who loved boys and girls!

Gene also discovered that she had an immense love for Jesus Christ. He realized that there was something different about Miss Ruth. Her quiet manner and the fact that she never drew attention to herself impressed him. She didn't get agitated or annoyed by the children in the neighborhood like most grown-ups did. Her ready smile and inner peace attracted Gene right away.

One of the first Bible stories Gene heard was about a boy named Joseph. Miss Ruth used a flannelgraph board and put up the figure of a boy dressed in a beautiful coat of many colors. As she finished the story she spoke of Jesus Christ who had died on the cross for our sins. She invited the children to ask him into their hearts to find forgiveness for their sins. Gene didn't respond that day, but he was curious to know more of the Candy Lady's stories.

Gene liked Miss Ruth. Sometimes he would go to the candy store in front of her house, but he *always* went to the Bible class in her basement. Often he arrived early so he could talk with her about the Bible stories. And often he would hang around after the other children left.

One day the Bible class ended with the singing of "Jesus Loves the Little Children of the World."

When the other children left, Miss Ruth spoke to Gene about Jesus' love for him. In her typical warm, loving manner she asked him if he would like to invite Jesus Christ into his life. "Gene, would you pray and thank Jesus for dying for your sins? Would you invite him into your life to be your Savior?"

Gene's heart had been prepared by Miss Ruth's love and the Holy Spirit's gentle conviction. He thought for a moment. "Yes, Miss Ruth. I'd like to do that today."

The old woman and the young boy prayed together that day, and Gene Ratley became a child of God. Two weeks later, just before his twelfth birthday, Gene was baptized to show the world about his new relationship with God.

That prayer in the Candy Lady's basement has since influenced more than just the eleven-year-old boy. Today people call him Pastor Gene Ratley, and he constantly tells others about the Savior he met many years ago in Miss Ruth's Bible class.

13

THE GOD BOYCOTT

If you watch football, you may have seen Todd
Peterson, one of the NFL's field-goal kickers, in
action. Currently playing for the Seattle Seahawks,
Todd has set many records for his team. Because of
his exemplary conduct off the field, the Seahawks
organization nominated Todd for the NFL Man of
the Year award in 1996.

But just a few years earlier, Todd Peterson was
a rowdy twenty-year-old; attending the University
of Georgia, he roamed the campus in search of
beer and sorority girls. He'd been raised in a
Christian home, involved in church, and president
of the Fellowship of Christian Athletes at his high
school. Throughout his later high school and
college years, however, Todd shied away from
fully committing his life to Jesus. Instead, he
preferred to follow his own desires—which meant
beer, parties, and girls.

That was why as a junior in college, Todd was boycotting the church retreat called "A Walk to Emmaus." The getaway was centered around spiritual growth, "with one weekend for men, the next for women." Todd's girlfriend had gone to the previous retreat and come back truly excited about God. Her parents and Todd's parents had also gone. All five of the retreat participators pushed Todd to go too—but he figured he had better things to do than spend a valuable weekend learning more about God.

The men were scheduled to leave for the retreat on Thursday. Wednesday night Todd's girlfriend made one last plea for Todd to join them. True to his self-imposed boycott, Todd refused, making it clear that he would *not* be going on the church retreat.

Thursday morning Todd awoke, still determined to avoid taking the "walk to Emmaus"; but he did feel guilty about the way he had expressed his opinion to his girlfriend the night before. Lying in bed, Todd felt bad for her and thought, *You know, I just should call her and apologize. I've been kind of a creep.* He dialed her number.

With a touch of hope, Todd's girlfriend asked, "Are you sure you won't go?" For the first time, Todd paused to consider the possibility. Having just transferred to Georgia, he was ineligible to play in that weekend's football game. *You know, I don't have anything better to do. Might as well go, otherwise I'm going to sit here and watch a college football game I can't play in.*

Todd ended his God boycott. "I guess I'll go."

Then he found out there weren't any spaces left on the retreat roster. He had waited too long to decide! But thirty minutes later, Todd's girlfriend called. Three people had cancelled their reservations, so Todd and two others could go on the retreat.

"It was just divine intervention!" Todd proclaims today. During that weekend the Spirit of God softened Todd Peterson. All through the weekend Todd could feel God gently breaking down the barriers of popularity, a self-serving lifestyle, and meaningless religious acts. It was then that Todd confronted his sin and called on Jesus to take over his life and change him from the inside out. With help from a few of the other men at the conference, Todd prayed and asked Jesus for forgiveness. He committed the rest of his life to serving God and following his lead.

Speaking of that weekend now, Todd says, "It was a long process, but I finally realized grace when I was twenty years old."

14

A NAZI SEPARATION

On the evening of July 26, 1939, little Hanna let
go of her mother's hand and climbed the steps to
the railroad car. The train slowly pulled away
from the station in Cologne, Germany. As the
locomotive gained speed and the train began to
race down the tracks, the anxiety in seven-year-old
Hanna grew.

"I am alone," she said to herself. Though many
other children and Red Cross workers filled the
car, the reality of what she had left behind
overwhelmed her.

Hanna had just taken her last glimpse of her
mother and father. She would never look into
their faces again or feel their embrace. She would
not hear them speak soft reassurances to her. Adolf
Hitler's Nazi regime would cruelly snatch their
lives away. Germany's borders had been slammed
shut to Jews, so they had to stay inside, where they

eventually died. In desperation Hanna's father had found a seat on the train for his daughter through the compassion of the Quakers and the Red Cross. Of the family, only Hanna would survive.

Hanna eventually found shelter in England, but the memories of her home and family frequently returned. *Why did I lose my parents? Why was I the only one saved? God, why me?*

In 1960, twenty-one years after the traumatic parting from her parents, Hanna sat in a pew in the Anglican church in the town of Horsham. Young evangelist Billy Graham was holding services there; he was the talk of the town! Curious, Hanna had gone to hear this powerful young preacher.

Reverend Graham began to speak. Hanna saw herself changing from curious bystander to attentive listener and active participant. Graham's message was becoming uncomfortably personal. She sat in the hard pew, struggling inside, remembering her past and brooding on her future.

Finally, the grief and bitterness that had built up over the years surfaced. *I cannot forgive those who have killed my parents.*

At that moment the Spirit of God brought a supernatural clarity to her. She understood the magnitude of Jesus' forgiveness of her own sin. Then the Holy Spirit opened her eyes to his ability to help her forgive her evil enemies. Outwardly Hanna appeared composed and still; inwardly profound changes took place. She knew that the words about Jesus Christ were true and that they were for her.

As the message drew to a close, Reverend

Graham invited his listeners to publicly receive Jesus Christ as Savior. "Come to the front and tell the world, 'I'm committing my life to Jesus Christ.'" But as powerful as the Lord's work had been within her, Hanna was reluctant to walk forward and disclose herself to so many people who knew her.

Eventually overcoming this fear, Hanna stood, then walked down the aisle to become a Christian. That walk represented her taking hold of Jesus and his forgiveness. And she found him taking hold of her, embracing her with his love and forgiveness. Joyfully she declared her trust in God. She found the awesome Lover from whom she would never be separated—not by Nazis, not by war, not by death, not by anything.

Today Hanna Miley exhibits an intense passion to share the transforming love of Christ with people who have never heard this Good News. She has known the power of forgiveness, and she is able to encourage others with this truth.

15

GRANDMOTHER
WALKER'S SAVIOR

If you had a grandmother like Isiah Oakes's
grandmother, you'd thank God like he does. Talk
to Isiah about his grandmother, and you'll see him
cry. Her imprint on his life is unmistakable. She
was one of those women who, like the smell of
freshly baked cookies, could stir a child's appetite.

But Grandmother Walker's aroma was much
greater than her cooking. *She* was the fragrance. It
was the perfume of Jesus' presence that permeated
her life and stirred young Isiah in the core of his
being. Isiah longed to know the Savior as Grandmother did. Many nights he would sit at her feet
and listen attentively as she described her
experiences walking with the Lord.

"As I sat listening to Grandmother tell of her
experiences," Isiah recalls, "I would literally weep.
Christ was so real to her, and she knew him in
such a personal way. I wanted to know him like

she did, but I didn't know how to make it happen."

When Isiah was a junior in high school, his grandmother took him to her church where the preacher, Dr. E. V. Hill, was conducting a revival service. The Spirit of God had been tilling the soil of Isiah's heart during all those days with Grandmother. Now, as a young man on his way to adulthood, Isiah's hunger for Jesus intensified.

At the close of the service, Dr. Hill gave an invitation, opening up the time to anyone who wanted to know Jesus. Because of his grandmother's example, Isiah knew that was what he wanted. Immediately, he walked down the aisle and prayed at the altar, committing his life to Jesus Christ.

In the days that followed he spent hours reading his Bible and praying to know Christ as his grandmother knew him. He was hounded with the nagging question, *Am I really saved?* He'd find himself praying, "Lord, if salvation is a gift, then why is it so hard to get to know you?" This turmoil continued for over two years.

In 1967, Isiah enrolled at Arizona State University on a track scholarship. There the Lord brought into Isiah's life students who were a part of Campus Crusade for Christ. One day they told him about the Christmas break retreat. "We want you to go with us."

Isiah began to think of all the reasons he couldn't go. "I don't have the money. I don't have transportation."

"Don't worry. We've got all those details already

cared for. Just be ready to go!" Reluctantly, Isiah consented to go.

The retreat proved to be a life-changing gift to Isiah. He knew God had orchestrated it just for him. Dr. Bill Bright spent the entire week on a theme addressing this young man's most pressing need: "The Assurance of My Salvation."

"Every day following a message I'd return to my room and ponder the truth I'd heard. I'd reread Scripture and think some more. This went on for the entire week."

Several weeks later the Spirit of God brought a profound enlightenment to Isiah. For the first time an overwhelming peace swept over him. An unswerving assurance that his salvation wasn't based on his efforts, but totally on the work of Christ, sprang to life. At that moment Isiah Oakes realized that God had kept his promise that day, years before, when the young high schooler knelt and prayed at the altar to commit his life to Christ.

Since that time Isiah has never doubted his security in Christ. He knows Grandmother Walker's Savior for himself.

16

A COLD NIGHT
IN TEXAS

"Fire up the engine, I'm freezing!" Jeff said.
David, dutiful friend that he was, turned the key
of his old Toyota Celica so he could crank up the
car's heater.

It was nearing three o'clock in the morning—
on a school night—but these two buddies were
busy talking. It was January 1982, and it was a
typically cold winter night in Fort Worth. But
Jefferson Scott had questions, and David had
answers. So they stayed in the parking lot of
David's church, sitting and talking in that chilly
tin car.

Jefferson Scott is now a Christian novelist who
writes thrillers along the lines of Tom Clancy and
John Grisham. But in January 1982, Jeff was a
sixteen-year-old high schooler whose deep love
was singing, not writing. He sang well enough to
make the "select" choir at his high school.

It was this interest in music that drew Jeff to the church parking lot that night. He didn't really care that much for church itself. Jeff's dad was a staunch secular humanist, and his mother was a Christian Scientist; with a strong intellectual background, neither of them thought much of Christianity. Still, they didn't object when David invited Jeff to an All Church Sing, and they didn't say no when Jeff decided to go.

During the All Church Sing Jeff noticed something different. The music sounded great, and the teenagers leading the singing looked like they were truly enjoying themselves. Jeff envied them and wished he could be up there with them—he wondered why he was not.

After the singing time David introduced Jeff to the music minister who had orchestrated it. They chatted awhile, and the minister asked Jeff what he thought about eternity. For all his intellectual upbringing, Jeff had no answer.

And that was why Jeff and David now sat in a freezing car, talking about Jesus, one telling the other about how Jesus provided a way for people to know God. A flood of questions poured from Jeff's heart, and with each answer, the Holy Spirit spoke to him.

It all seemed so new and wonderful to Jeff. "I instantly knew it was right and knew it was for me. I accepted it as the words of God and not of men. At 3:00 A.M. that morning, I invited Jesus Christ onto the throne of my heart."

It has been nearly two decades since that invitation, but Jesus still sits on the throne of Jeff's heart. Through his novels and other writing, Jefferson Scott explains to others the good news about Jesus that he first heard on a cold January night, deep in the heart of Texas.

17

THE PROPHECY

George McCluskey is dead, that much is true. But his children and grandchildren still remember the man as well as the prophecy he related to his family.

George was a praying man who spent hours a day speaking and listening to God. Often, the topic of George's daily petitions was his family—specifically, that his offspring would all know and serve Jesus. He prayed with passion, concern, and a heart moved by the heart of God.

It was during one of these daily prayers that the prophecy came about. George *felt* rather than *heard* God speaking to him. In a way that can't fully be described, George felt certain God was making this promise: Every member of George's family for the next four generations would serve Jesus Christ and honor him with their lives.

That was George's prophecy and what he held on to all his life, up to the day of his death.

Four generations after George McCluskey, little Jim was born into the family. Jim was the great-grandson of George. Jim's dad was a pastor and a traveling preacher. God was at work in little Jim even when Jim was only one year old. Though he couldn't speak, Jim insisted on "praying" with his parents, imitating the sounds he heard as his parents talked with God.

At three years old, Jim had a meeting he would never forget. It was a Sunday evening, and he accompanied his family to a church service in which his father was the preacher. At the end of the sermon, Jim's dad invited anyone from the congregation to come to the front and pray at the altar to receive Jesus Christ's love and forgiveness. About fifteen or twenty people responded, and Jim was one of them.

"I remember the occasion clearly . . ." says Jim, over a half century later. "It is overwhelming for me to think of that event today. Imagine the King of the universe, the Creator of all heaven and earth, caring about an insignificant kid barely out of toddlerhood! It makes no sense, but I know it happened."

Jim is an adult now, and God is still fulfilling the prophecy he gave George McCluskey. Perhaps you've heard of little Jim. He went on to become a noted psychologist and a marriage and family counselor. He also served on the staff of the University of Southern California School of Medicine as well as the Children's Hospital of Los

Angeles. For the past few decades, he has been a strong advocate of Christian family values, active in governmental affairs and advisor to three U.S. presidents.

But you probably know this man best for the educational organization he founded, Focus on the Family, and by his professional name: Dr. James Dobson.

18

BROTHER'S KEEPER

I can't handle any more of this, John said to himself.
*My world is falling apart, and I don't know what I
believe or value anymore. I'm not even sure that I believe
that God exists, but if he does I sure need him. I've got
to get away to think.*

John Mills packed his VW van and headed for
northern California to visit his brother, David.

John's life had started off well. He grew up in a
stable home with parents who taught strong moral
values. He attended religious education classes at
church and even served as an altar boy. A deep
respect for God and the name of Jesus Christ were
instilled in him early in life. The nuns at church
had trained him to bow his head whenever he
passed a church or heard the name of Jesus
mentioned.

John was devout in this belief system. He
genuinely believed that Jesus Christ was the Son of

God and that he had died for the sins of the world. *But a critical element was missing.* John Mills failed to grasp the significance of what Christ's death meant *for him.* He knew *about* Christ, but he didn't know him.

As John entered his teens he encountered pressures to "enjoy life." Though he still held respect for the name of Jesus Christ, his belief system began to erode. When he enrolled at the University of Arizona, the opportunity for parties, alcohol, and drugs subtly seduced him. Religion just couldn't compete.

Marrying Judy was another thing that had started out with so much promise. But John's immaturity and self-centered attitude made good communication difficult. Judy was self-disciplined and morally righteous, and she resisted his efforts to "loosen her up." Well, John didn't intend to change. So the cancer set in, and the marriage began to die.

John became unsettled. Outwardly he appeared confident and sure; inwardly he was anxious and searching. His life completely fell apart when Judy announced their three-year marriage was ending. "You don't love me anymore, so I've filed for a divorce." That decision devastated John.

God had John's attention. His heart was ready to hear more about Jesus. The trip to California to visit his brother gave him lots of time to mull over the issues. And his brother, David, was a Christian who cared about John's spiritual condition.

One evening shortly after John had arrived, he and David had a long conversation about the great void in John's life. David urged his brother to read selections from the book of Romans as a foundation for further talks. John followed his brother's advice, but he still didn't understand what he read.

"It just doesn't make sense. It seems to be a string of unconnected sentences." So again they explored the Scriptures, and David patiently explained that Jesus was God's Son, sent to earth; that Jesus died on the cross to pay the penalty for sin; and that he returned from the dead with the offer of eternal life to all who would believe in him.

Later that night in the solitude of his bedroom, John's resistance began to crumble. He had been trying to fight for his own way but was coming to the end of this agonizing battle. He knew that his stubborn, self-serving life must be transformed by Jesus Christ. Ironically, in losing that battle he was rescued for eternity.

John is still working through the consequences of poor decisions in his past, but he tries to live each day in the transforming grace of God.

19

LAUGHING MATTERS

Joe Gautier (pronounced "go-CHAY") is a comedian-singer who likes to spout deeply theological thoughts like these:

"My favorite Scripture is this: 'A fool's mouth deserves a beating.' So what I like to do is hang out with a fool. And carry a blunt object with me."

"I realized finally why gorillas have such big nostrils. They have big fingers."

"God gave me this song, but I made the dance up myself."

"Hey, that's my ministry," Gautier explains. Mixing faith with humor, Gautier is one of the voices in Christian comedy. A performer in both Christian and mainstream outlets, Gautier has shared the stage with such artists as Michael W. Smith, Mark Lowry, Hammer, The Pointer Sisters, Amy Grant, and CeCe Winans.

But when Joey G. was five years old, life was

no laughing matter. His mother had just been taken to the hospital to give birth to Joe's sister. A family friend, Wilma Wild, took charge of Joe, and soon they were headed to the hospital as well.

Seeing his mother rushed off like that had shaken the young boy. Riding in the back of Wilma's Volvo, Joe began feeling fearful, to the point where he thought his mother might die in childbirth. He spoke his fear.

"I'm really afraid. I don't want my mom to die. And if I died, I would want to be with my mom if she dies."

Wilma calmly replied, "Well, Joey, you don't have to be afraid. You can ask Jesus to come into your heart."

Then she explained the story of salvation and how even five-year-olds could accept Jesus and be granted eternal life in heaven with him. Joey G. knew exactly what he wanted after hearing that story.

"I want to do that."

Wilma took a short detour on the way to the hospital, stopping by heaven's door with a preschooler who was thinking of eternity.

"We prayed right there in the backseat of the Volvo," says Joe today, with gratitude that the heavenly Father took notice of his kid fears.

A TWO-FOR-ONE
CLEANSING

The pavement radiated heat that day. The year was
1987, and it was another blistering Sunday morning
in Tempe, Arizona.

Eleven-year-old Brad Chaney slipped into the
restroom at Grace Community Church between
the Sunday school hour and the morning worship
service. *Just enough time for a quick refreshment,* he
thought.

Brad's family had been attending Grace for
about a year. During that time he was impressed
with an elderly gentleman who was one of the
usual greeters at the Sunday morning worship
service. Brad didn't remember the man's name, but
he never forgot the friendly smile that spread across
the man's face. His welcome was warm and
inviting. *I can see Jesus in him,* Brad often thought.

On this particular Sunday, Brad stood washing
his hands in the church restroom when the

welcomer himself entered, greeting the boy with his typical warmth. But the words he uttered next caught the youngster off guard.

"Son, have you ever taken Jesus Christ as your personal Savior? He died for your sins, you know."

Brad had heard about Jesus' death on the cross since he was in the third grade. He had been taught the message behind the man's question. Lately he had thought about his own relationship with the Lord. But no one had ever addressed the question to him personally. There'd never been a one-to-one encounter.

After a quick thought, Brad replied, "No, sir, I've never done that."

"Would you like to do it now?"

Brad knew immediately. "Yes, I would."

So the old man and young boy bowed their heads in the restroom, and Brad admitted to God that he was a sinner and asked for forgiveness through the grace of Jesus Christ.

"The Lord saved me in the most unlikely place and in the most unlikely way," Brad says now. "I gave my life to Christ and left the bathroom washed, from head to foot, both inside and out. I walked out of the bathroom saying to myself, 'Now I know I'm saved. . . . I'll go to heaven when I die.'"

21

FOUR-YEAR-OLD
THEOLOGY

Something was on Johnston Camp's mind this
Sunday, something that was even distracting him
from what Dad called a "Beatitude Meal"—the
McDonald's Happy Meal he was eating for Sunday
lunch. The preschooler turned to his father. "Dad,
what's a sin nature?"

Rarely does a four-year-old ask questions about
theology. Steve Camp was taken by surprise and
choked down a bit of his burger. "Johnston, where
did you hear that?"

"I heard you mention it to someone at church.
What does it mean?"

Carefully Steve explained to Johnston how sin
entered the world because of Adam and Eve's failure
in the Garden of Eden; since then, every person is
born with a tendency to sin, something we call a
"sin nature." Steve explained how Jesus came to

earth, died by crucifixion, and rose from the dead to defeat that sin nature and save us from sin.

There was a moment of silence, then Johnston looked up. "Did Jesus have to die for me?"

"Yes, Son. He had to because of that sin nature."

The wheels were obviously turning in young Johnston's head. He was concentrating on this new information. The little boy had one more question to ask.

"He had to die for me. But did he *want* to die for me?"

Steve reached out to his son and marveled at the boy's innocent grasp of God. "Yes, Johnston. Not only did Jesus *have* to die for you, but he *wanted* to die for you. His love held him to Calvary's tree."

Johnston nodded, ending the conversation and finishing his meal. Dad and son got in the car and began the drive home.

But something was still bothering Johnston. He broke the silence. "You know, Dad, I love the Lord. I would like to know him as my Lord and Savior. Could I receive the Lord?"

Steve Camp remembers with joy what happened next. "I had the privilege of pulling off to the side of the road and leading my son to the Lord!"

When the prayer ended, Johnston smiled at Dad. "Does this make me now a Christian soldier?"

"Yes, Johnston, it does." Then he handed the little soldier his new sword—Dad's own Bible.

SMILES

His smile first caught Tressa's attention. She wasn't looking for a boyfriend—she already had one. But fourteen-year-old Tressa Kitchens was always in the market for a friend, and something about that guy's smile made her think he was the kind of guy who'd be a friend for life. Besides, Tressa was feeling a little homesick. It was only the second day of youth camp, and she was ready to go home! But here came Mike, smiling at her.

"Hey, we're going to go out for a walk around the campgrounds. Want to come along?" Mike motioned to a few friends.

Tressa was happy to be included in a group of friends. Of course she'd go! Besides, she had to find out more about that grin draped on her new friend's face.

As the week of camp continued, Tressa and Mike started hanging out. They ate meals together, went to the church services and Bible studies together, and spent free time playing Ping-Pong or tossing a Frisbee. It seemed that Mike had this contagious happiness that drew people to him, and he was always happy to welcome Tressa into his group of friends. It was medicine for Tressa's homesick soul.

As their friendship grew, Mike and Tressa talked often about God, life, and happiness. "He kept asking me tough questions!" Tressa remembers.

"Where do you think you'll go when you die?" he'd ask. "What do you hope to do with your life? Do you think there's more to this life than what you're experiencing now?" With every question, Mike would return to one theme: Jesus.

Tressa enjoyed those conversations because she could work out her thoughts and beliefs; she enjoyed being on the receiving end of Mike's questions. Their talks challenged her. But really, that was all. It wasn't like she needed to become a Christian or anything.

Or did she?

On the last night of the camp, Tressa, Mike, and several other friends sat in the final church service. "I chatted during the whole service." Tressa laughs. "I never heard a word of the sermon."

Still, at the end of the sermon something began to grip her heart. The week's conversations and challenges welled up inside Tressa. The music director led the student congregation in an old hymn, "The Savior Is Waiting."

Tressa was silent. Something was happening; she could feel it. "I felt an incredible warmth come over me, and I had the sensation of pins and needles going up and down my back. In that moment a small voice said to me, 'Go down to the front. I want you to commit your life to me.'"

Turning to the one person she knew would understand, she said to Mike, "Will you walk down with me?"

Mike nodded, and together they approached the front. Kneeling at the camp's altar, Tressa turned her life over to Jesus that night, inviting him into her heart forever.

Tressa eventually lost contact with Mike, but she never forgot the easy grin that first drew her to Jesus.

23

RELIGIOUS REGRETS

If only I could find a simpler, more peaceful life, Lalo
Vargas thought to himself as he sat in the solitude
of his room. Coming to San Andres University in
La Paz, Bolivia, was exciting at the beginning. He
was free from family control and free to party. But
by 1987 he was nearing graduation, and the life of
"wine, women, and song" was stagnating.

A vague feeling like conscience weighed him
down. "I felt an intense need to be more simple,
and I knew that I needed to be cleansed within
from something dark and dirty. But I wasn't strong
enough in myself to do it."

His natural response was to return to his
family's religious tradition—the Roman Catholic
Church. Daily Lalo would enter the sanctuary,
recite a number of prayers, and promise the Virgin
Mary that he would end the evil lifestyle he'd
adopted.

Then he'd go out and fail miserably again, repeating the cycle of sin that enslaved him.

I'm trapped in the clutches of sin, and the load of guilt is suffocating me! he thought. *It's growing heavier every day.* He thought often of death—and those thoughts terrorized him. At church he'd repent, but when he left the sanctuary, the nightmare would continue.

In August 1988 Lalo received his degree in architecture amid family celebration. To his family he looked happy, but Lalo knew the double life he had skillfully hidden from them. He felt unsettled and restless but did not know how to change.

One October evening Lalo stopped to see his Aunt Diva. She was a faithful follower of Jesus Christ and attended an "evangelical" church. He tended to avoid contact with Aunt Diva because he feared that she might pressure him to change his lifestyle. He was also anxious that she might change his conceptions about God—something his family and friends would oppose. Diva's "evangelical" religion was not the religion of his fathers.

Still, she was his aunt, so Lalo stopped by to chat with her. After a few minutes Aunt Diva said, "I have to go out tonight. Come with me."

"Where are you going?" Lalo asked cautiously.

"To church. Come with me. There's a campaign tonight."

In spite of Lalo's anxiety about the church and his appearance, he joined Aunt Diva that night. The warmth and friendliness of the people disarmed him, and they took a genuine interest in him. Lalo was impressed by their sincerity.

The thing that caught Lalo totally off guard, though, was the singing. He was unprepared for that type of worship. "I was surrounded by the sense of God's presence, but it created a powerful tension within. I knew that if I ran from this place I would be rejecting the help I so desperately needed. But I dreaded the commitment I knew I needed to make. So I sat quietly."

The congregational singing opened Lalo's heart, and the pastor's message penetrated it. Afterward the pastor invited anyone to come pray for Jesus to enter his or her life. Lalo was faced with a momentous decision that caused him to tremble. He sweated. His heart said "Yes," but his mind resolutely said "No!"

Finally he said no to his pride and surrendered himself to Christ's love. In that instant Lalo felt his life being filled with hope. The presence of the Lord that he had sensed during the singing now filled Lalo with joy. In the weeks, months, and years to come, Lalo's new experience with Jesus Christ enabled him to change the patterns of guilt and sin that had once ruled his life.

Eleven years later Lalo paused to reflect on that moment of salvation he'd experienced, thanks to Aunt Diva. "After eleven years . . . I still have difficult times, but the difference is that I am not alone. I have a great family and an even greater Father who will never forsake me. He continues to give me that faith, hope, and love that he gave me that October night in 1988."

24

FREE AT LAST

When Tony Nappa was eighteen months old, he broke his foot in that world-renowned sport commonly called "jumping on the bed." (Though he didn't actually break his foot until he jumped *off* the bed.)

Tony would not be deterred from the jumping games by something as annoying as a little blue cast on his leg. The resourceful toddler learned to jump on the bed again within days—cast and all! Eventually the leg healed.

Three years later, Tony's mom found him playing his favorite bed-jumping games on her bed. This time Tony had added a new dimension to his sport—rap music. Other mothers might have frowned, turned down the stereo, and lectured their child on safety and musical taste, but Tony's mom was special. Putting down her laundry basket, she cranked up the stereo and joined her son in dancing and bouncing on the bed.

If the neighbors had been listening closely that day, they would have heard the stereo loudly playing and dc Talk joyously rapping words from an old Negro spiritual, "Free, free, I'm free at last! Thank God Almighty, I'm free at last!" They also might have heard laughter and clapping and squeaking bedsprings.

When the song ended, Tony's mom turned to her son and, feeling playful and a bit out of breath, asked, "Tony, are you free?"

Instead of ignoring the question, four-and-a-half-year-old Tony embraced the question, pausing to think. While his mom turned the stereo back down to a respectable level, Tony's mind thought back to a "Wordless Book" his parents had shared with him.

The Wordless Book was really a simple thing: five pages, each a different color, and no text anywhere. Both Mom and Dad had explained it to Tony several times.

"The first page is black," they'd say. "Black for sin, which covers our hearts and lives.

"The next page is red. Red for Jesus' blood, which he shed on the cross and which has the power to wash away our sins.

"Third is the white page. White, because when we ask Jesus into our heart and ask him to forgive our sins, he makes us fresh and clean—white as snow!

"Fourth is gold. That's because heaven's streets

are made of gold—and that's the wonderful place Jesus has prepared for those who follow him.

"The last page is green. Green for growing, so we can remember to grow in our relationship with God each day until he finally takes us to heaven."

Black, red, white, gold, green, Tony thought. *Black, red, white . . . Black, red . . . Black. Black!*

Turning to his mother, Tony asked, "Is my heart still black with sin?" Mom sat on the bed next to Tony and gently explained that everyone's heart is black until Jesus washes it clean and sets the person free.

Tony replied, "I want to ask Jesus into my heart, to make it not black, and to make me free." Then, surprisingly, he asked his mother to leave the room so he could ask Jesus into his heart privately. She obeyed his request. A few minutes later, Tony strode into the living room with a smile on his face. He said he had asked Jesus into his heart, and now it was white as snow. That evening when Tony's dad came home from work, Tony reported the good news to him.

The Bible teaches that heaven celebrates when a soul is rescued from sin. On the night of June 3, 1994, the Nappa household joined that celebration, cranking up the stereo as they sang along with dc Talk:

"Free, free, I'm free at last! Thank God Almighty, I'm free at last!"

25

SCARED INTO JESUS' ARMS

"Son, we're going to the revival at First Baptist in Fabens this Friday night!" Jerry's mother said. "Your dad won't have to work on Saturday, so he said we could go."

That was good news to twelve-year-old Jerry Leatherwood. What boy wouldn't want to get in on those pies and cakes they served before the meeting? Besides, many of his friends would be there, and that was always fun.

For the past year Jerry's family had been attending church. He'd heard about Jesus Christ many times, but he didn't think he was ready to go to heaven. At church he would feel like he needed to commit his life to Jesus, but then he'd think to himself, *Hold on now! Don't make a hasty decision. You've got your whole life ahead of you. If you just hold on a few minutes those guilt feelings will go away. Don't be in such a rush. There's plenty of time.* With such reasoning, Jerry would resist the persistent, gentle calling of the Holy Spirit.

When the Leatherwoods got to First Baptist that Saturday night, the place was packed. About four hundred people were crowded in. The singing started, and Jerry began to enjoy himself—until his mom leaned over and said quietly, "I didn't want to miss tonight. The evangelist is preaching on 'Hell. Is It a Real Place?'" Suddenly Jerry didn't feel so comfortable.

The evangelist stood, opened his Bible, and began preaching. Jerry felt compelled to listen. Fear welled up within him, and it seemed that the preacher kept looking right at him! Sitting next to the aisle gave Jerry a good view of the preacher, but it also gave the preacher a great view of him. The longer the message continued, the stronger Jerry's fear grew. Soon Jerry was genuinely scared, and he knew that hell was something he did not want to experience.

Finally, the message ended, and everyone stood to sing the invitational hymn. Jerry grasped the back of the pew in front of him and held on for dear life. His hands were shaking. His heart felt like it was going to jump right out of his chest. This was one night when he could hear the voice of God's Spirit clearly and convincingly.

Then Jerry heard his mother's kind voice. "I'll go with you if you want me to."

He responded almost immediately. "No, I'll go by myself." The next thing Jerry knew he was running down the aisle with tears streaming down his cheeks. The evangelist met him in the front of the church and welcomed him joyfully. "Do you want to ask Jesus to come into your life? Do you want him to forgive your sins?" he asked.

"Yes I do. I really want to do it," Jerry cried. The evangelist prayed with the boy, and to Jerry it seemed as though a thousand pounds were lifted from his back. In that moment Jerry knew he was saved from the terrors of hell, and his fear of dying evaporated.

But it wasn't just fear that kept Jerry faithful to his new commitment. Soon he discovered how much Jesus loved him and that Jesus' love could overcome all fear. Today Jerry Leatherwood is retired, but he stays active in his church and has lived many years as a man committed to Jesus Christ. He dedicated his life to deepening his relationship with God through reading the Bible, praying, and doing his best to live as he thinks Jesus would want him to live.

As he recalled that night many years ago, he said, "Hell is a terrible place, and I was literally scared into the arms of Jesus. How I thank my mom for seeing the conviction I was under and gently asking me if I wanted her to go with me. I might have waited and heard the other voice telling me that I had plenty of time to wait."

26

GOD FINDS AN
ORPHAN

This is an American religion, thought Le Thai, as a
fellow student at Texas Tech University told him
of Jesus Christ. *It's not as personable and intimate as
the ancestor worship I've experienced in my homeland.*

So instead of Jesus, Le chose to continue
praying to his deceased grandmother, who had
loved him dearly, and he took comfort in praying
to his mother, who had passed away when he was
a child. That was what he had always been taught,
and that was what he believed.

From his birth in Saigon, South Vietnam, Le
Thai's life was rooted in Buddhism. "My family
would go to the pagoda to worship, especially
during the Tet holidays. We would burn incense
and ask for good luck. We worshiped our
ancestors.

"Perched on top of our house was an ornate
altar with statues of Buddha and pictures of our

ancestors. Annually my extended family would gather and commemorate the death of my grandmother by burning incense in front of an altar and by asking for her protection over our family. While these practices may seem strange to you, memories of those days bring back many happy feelings."

When Le was seventeen years old, his father sent him to the United States to go to college. Money was always a problem during these school years. His father had no surplus, so Le worked two jobs in the summers to eke out a living. He also changed schools a few times, ending up at Texas Tech University.

It was there he first heard about Jesus Christ. But the Vietnamese culture had powerfully shaped Le's thinking. In his homeland major decisions were rarely made individually. Decisions were made by the consensus of the whole family. And his family would not tolerate his converting to a foreign religion.

Then in 1975, South Vietnam fell to the communist forces of North Vietnam. Overnight he lost both family and country. His father couldn't escape and died soon afterward.

"The Christmas season in 1975 was especially difficult for me," Le remembers. "The dormitory was deserted of all my American friends. Foreign students were allowed to stay on campus, but meal service was not provided. With no place to go, nothing to eat, and no home to visit, we ended up crowding around the TV set. Most of us were a homesick bunch, thinking of happier days we'd spent with family and friends back home."

Le faced an uncertain future. While other foreign students would finish their studies and return home, he could not return to his homeland. He was an orphan without a country. And though he was living in a land of abundance, Le was barely surviving on a poverty-level income. Cold pork and beans from a can were his staple.

But an even deeper hunger gnawed at Le. He was starved for love. How he longed to be back home with his father and able to speak with him one last time! Even his prayers to his dead mother and grandmother brought no relief. Le was truly alone in the world.

During the Christmas holiday a college friend stopped by the dorm, inviting Le to his home for Christmas. The thought of home-cooked food excited Le. And to be in a home with a gracious, kind family . . . Le accepted the invitation without hesitating!

Upon arriving at the friend's home, he was immediately struck by the warmth and friendship the family displayed. They even presented him with a Christmas gift—a new pair of pants. In that loving environment, Le's friend shared with him the true meaning of Christmas, telling him the good news of Jesus' birth, death, and resurrection. Le was still unsure.

The two friends returned to school, and over the next few days they read and discussed the Gospel of John. This part of the Bible intrigued Le. He pondered and questioned what he had read. *I*

wonder if God is real and if Jesus is truly God. I wonder
if he would help me. It's hard for me to accept the
miracles of Jesus I'm reading about. My scientific
mind-set makes it hard to believe that they are more than
fairy tales.

But God's Spirit had been cultivating the soil of
Le's heart and removing roadblocks. He realized
that neither Buddha nor his ancestors had helped
him, and it was now time to decide for himself
whom he would follow.

So on January 8, 1976, Le Thai bowed his head
and prayed—not to his grandmother or to his
mother—but to his eternal Father in heaven, the
Father who sent his Son, Jesus, to save people—to
save Le Thai.

Le Thai was no longer an orphan.

You might wonder what has happened to Le
since 1976. Today he is an anesthesiologist, a
student at Phoenix Seminary, and an active member
of his church. And God has given him a family of
his own—a wife and two sons he loves dearly.

27

BACKSTAGE PASS

Ron Rhodes sat backstage, preparing for his performance. He'd done this kind of thing dozens of times. Being on stage was nothing new. Still, there was always that flutter in the pit of the stomach, that nagging worry that something might go wrong. But Ron was a professional. He knew he'd go out there, and he knew he'd pull off yet another rock concert victory. At least, he hoped so.

It was the 1970s: the time when disco ruled, but rock-'n'-roll wasn't far behind. In his early twenties, Ron was already on track for Hollywood fame. He and his siblings had formed a group, The Rhodes Kids, and were patiently working their way up the music industry ladder. They had already performed on the *Merv Griffin Show*.

Their success did not go unnoticed. When Christian singer-actor Pat Boone and his family needed an opening act, they contacted The

Rhodes Kids to perform with them. That's how Ron met Pat's wife, Shirley.

After working together for a while, Shirley and Ron became friends, and it wasn't long before Shirley introduced Ron to the one true Friend, Jesus.

Ron listened intently to what Shirley said. When she finished speaking, Ron knew he had to have this new life. For the first time in his life, the power of a personal relationship with Christ had been made real to him, and he craved that relationship more than fame, more than applause, more than anything.

Shirley led Ron in a prayer, helping this performer understand his need for Jesus. At that moment the applause of heaven drowned out the applause at the concert hall. Ron Rhodes had become a Christian.

Twenty years later, Ron is not performing in crowded music halls. He's making his voice known in theological and ministry circles. He frequently cohosts the radio talk show *Bible Answer Man*. Ron shares his wisdom with others via books and as an editor of the *Christian Research Journal*.

But for all his accomplishments, Ron Rhodes is proudest of the privilege he had of leading his own two children, David and Kylie, into a relationship with Jesus. The gift that Shirley Boone once shared with a young man named Ron has now become a gift for his children as well.

28

COCA-COLA
COMMITMENTS

The two seventeen-year-old girls sat across from each other at McDonald's, sipping their Cokes. A little booklet lay open between them. As Lisa Bonet sipped, she could tell that her friend Cathy was nervous.

What is in that booklet that makes her so uptight? Lisa wondered.

Lisa and Cathy met as sophomores, when Lisa moved from southern California to Phoenix, Arizona. Lisa was bummed because she'd left so many friends behind, and she felt very alone in the new high school. But then she met Cathy, and the two of them "clicked" right away. One bonding point was that they were the only two girls who could beat all the guys at racquetball!

As Lisa and Cathy's friendship grew, they talked about many things. Then one day at McDonald's, Cathy brought up the topic of God. She asked questions that Lisa couldn't answer. Lisa knew she believed in God. Someone mighty *had* to exist to create the plants, animals, and people she saw all around her.

But one question Cathy asked unsettled her. "Lisa, if you could know God personally, would you want to?"

"Of course, wouldn't everyone?" Lisa blurted out without thinking. She sensed that Cathy knew more than she was saying. Lisa's mind wandered back to when she had attended church with her grandmother three years earlier. It was a special event because her grandmother was funny, and she brought M&M's to nibble on during the service. She also gave Lisa a Bible.

Lisa tried to read the Bible but could not understand what it was saying. She finally decided that people went to church to get the "scoop" from the preacher. He probably had a connection with God, but Lisa knew that she didn't. In fact, she had never met a person who claimed to know the Lord personally. Now Cathy said that even a teenager could know him. And the mysterious little booklet between them told how.

Putting their Cokes aside for a moment, Cathy nervously began to read through the "Four Spiritual Laws" tract, explaining step-by-step how a person could know Jesus Christ personally. Lisa was amazed. She'd never heard anything like this before! She became more and more fascinated.

Cathy read the final sentence. Lisa looked into her face and asked, "What's the next step? Can I pray that prayer?" She could tell by the look on

Cathy's face—and by her shaking hands—that Cathy had never shared such an important decision with anyone.

"Do you really want to pray?" asked Cathy. "Do you want to ask Jesus Christ into your heart right now? Do you want to pray this prayer?"

Lisa's responded enthusiastically. "YES! Right here, right now. Why not?"

The two girls bowed their heads. Lisa prayed to Jesus, asking him to enter her life right there in the booth at McDonald's. Finally, Lisa Bonet knew that she too had a "connection" with God. She knew he was her Father, and that changed her forever.

Many years have passed since that night, but one thing about Lisa has stayed the same: an enthusiastic, personal relationship with Jesus Christ. Because she remembers how things might be different if Cathy had decided NOT to share the Good News with her, Lisa is devoted to telling every new friend she meets about God's love through Jesus Christ.

29

FOOTBALL AND GIRLS—
IN THAT ORDER

A lot was happening in the world in 1968: the
Vietnam War, the space race, assassinations, the
hippie movement, the civil rights movement, and
demonstrations on college campuses. It was a time
of social upheaval and monumental events.

But for seventeen-year-old John Croyle, only
two things mattered: football and girls—in that
order.

A defensive starter on his high school football
team in Gadsden, Alabama, John was only a junior
when college scholarship offers started coming.
Since he also played basketball, John had his pick
of schools across the country. He would go on
to play defensive end for Alabama's coach, Paul
"Bear" Bryant, winning a national championship
for Alabama in his senior year of college.

But on this day in 1968, he was still a high
school junior dreaming of the future. When he

heard that a REAL football player, a pro for the Dallas Cowboys, was coming to town to speak, John knew he had to be there. So what if it was a religious thing, some meeting put on by a group called Campus Crusade for Christ? Maybe there would be some cute girls there too.

On the night of the meeting, John casually joined the crowd to hear what this Cowboys player had to say. Sure enough, he noticed some cute girls there. John made plans to pick up one of the girls he saw. After all, who could resist Gadsden's budding star football player, muscular and good-looking?

He shifted his focus toward the speaker—and found himself caught up in the story. This player was telling about how he had grown up, about the day Christ broke through to him and the difference that relationship had made. The words he spoke made John think and totally distracted him from his pick-up plans.

Then out of nowhere a man in the audience came over to John. Looking straight at John, he asked, "If you were to die tonight, where would you spend eternity?"

John was flabbergasted. "I evaluated what the man said. I was seventeen years old; I was a junior in high school; I could play college and had college scholarships in football and basketball to any college I wanted to go to. But I didn't have an answer to that man's question."

In frustration, John lashed out verbally at the man who had asked the question. "Mister, I don't know. Just leave me alone!"

The stranger stepped away briefly, then returned. "Jesus Christ can give you peace." Then he was gone.

When the meeting ended, John Croyle went straight home. There the turmoil inside him turned into a stuttered prayer. "God, Jesus, Bible, Holy Ghost—whoever it is I'm supposed to be talking to—come in and change me and make me what you want me to be."

Jesus heard that simple prayer and answered it. Three decades later, John is still praying to God, though with more clarity. He knows the answer to the question that man asked. John Croyle is going to heaven, and he plans on bringing along with him as many people as he can.

That simple prayer back in 1968 gave John a new priority over football and girls: Jesus Christ. Because of that priority, John forewent the opportunity for a lucrative career as a professional football player, choosing instead to start a ranch home in Alabama for orphaned and abused children. To date, he's influenced over thirteen hundred children in this Christian home environment and helped many come to know Jesus like he has.

For John, that's worth more than all the football contracts in the world.

30

DRINKERS AND THINKERS
IN COLORADO

Martin was so drunk he didn't even notice when his friends left—even though they were his only way home. Finally, at closing time—2:00 A.M. for this Colorado bar—Martin realized he was alone. Worse yet, he was still miles and miles from his home in nearby Grand Lakes.

What could he do? Braving the night, he started walking and thinking.

An accomplished philosophy student, Martin Nagy spent plenty of time thinking. *Does God exist? And if he doesn't exist, then what standards do I live my life by? And what purpose is my life?*

Studying such great thinkers as Nietzsche, Camus, and Sartre only left Martin more confused than ever. That was why he'd moved to Grand Lakes, Colorado, the year before—to spend time alone contemplating the existence of God and to reconsider some of Kierkegaard's ideas. That had

been August of 1981. Now, in May of 1982,
Martin had decided he would give up, embrace
the philosophy of an agnostic, and assume God was
either nonexistent or impotent.

So tonight Martin walked and thought and tried
to clear his fuzzy, alcohol-muddled brain. After
traveling seven or eight miles, he came upon a
hotel owned by a friend. Martin stayed there for
the night.

Back home in Grand Lakes the next day,
Martin made a decision: no more hanging out
in bars. Drinking made him feel terrible and
apathetic. At home, then, he must find something
to do while his friends went out barhopping. What
to do? Why not read a book?

Passing by his philosophy texts, Martin reached
for a book his sister had sent him. A nun in a
Catholic order, she frequently reminded her
brother that she was praying for him, and she had
sent him a Christian book called *The Helper* by
Catherine Marshall. The book was filled with
testimonies of how God's Holy Spirit had worked
in people's lives.

Martin was transfixed by what he read. Was this
true? Was God really alive and working in the lives
of people just like him? Martin realized that the
Holy Spirit was doing more than just touching
other people's lives. While Martin read the book,
the Holy Spirit touched Martin's heart.

When he finished the book, Martin paused. He
knew he wanted this Holy Spirit he had read
about. So he prayed, asking God to come in, take

over, and give him the power to live as a Christian.

Martin recalls that for the rest of his time in Grand Lakes, he spent a few hours each morning praying and reading the Bible. "The words of the Bible seemed to leap off the page at me! I'd lose track of time and read the Bible for hours, sitting on the edge of my seat with excitement."

Martin never got intoxicated again because he was filled with the Spirit.

31

SOWING SALVATION
SEEDS

Mark Yule dialed Carla's number and waited to hear his sister's voice. *She's one person who knows me. I've got to talk to someone,* he thought. He'd been phoning her a lot lately to talk over all that had been going on in his life.

"Carla, I'm down in the dumps. My life's not going anywhere, and I feel so confused. I don't know what to do."

Carla replied without hesitation. "Mark, I think you know that it's a spiritual issue. So much of what you're seeking is found in Christ. Why don't you commit your life to him?"

Mark knew his sister was telling the truth. The series of events that had transpired lately made it clear. When Mark and his girlfriend attended the Billy Graham Crusade a few months ago, he began to think about his life. Listening to Dr. Graham made him aware that he needed something more to live for, something to give his life meaning and a purpose. As a senior at Arizona State University, he felt ready to face the world—almost. He knew something was missing.

One day at school a Campus Crusade guy came into his dorm room and lectured him about "four spiritual laws." This guy was too aggressive, and he pushed Mark to pray a prayer. Mark wasn't ready for that. Still, he had made Mark think.

The concert of Handel's *Messiah* also made him think. His girlfriend was in the choir so he went with her to rehearsal. As he sat in the back, he was strangely drawn to the message of the music. It was as though the real Messiah was calling him.

But Mark had always believed he was the captain of his own ship. *I'm a logical guy. I can make my own way. Anything is possible if you work hard enough, right?* If only things had worked out the way he'd planned! Mark dated the same girl for three years, thinking one day they'd eventually get married. Instead, they broke up.

Now he was due to graduate from ASU. But he didn't know what he wanted to do, where he wanted to go, or with whom he wanted to associate. Mark was beginning to think that he needed a new pilot. That's why he kept calling Carla. And that's why she kept pointing him to Jesus Christ.

This time, however, Mark hung up the phone and he knew—really *knew*—that he must follow Carla's words. He waited quietly, then alone by the phone he bowed his head in prayer. He confessed his sins, asked for Christ's forgiveness, and resolved to capitulate to Jesus Christ.

In a clear and wonderful way the Lord began to give new direction to Mark's life. He grew in wisdom as he read the Bible and eventually assumed leadership in his church. Today he is on the pastoral staff of a new church. Whenever a troubled soul calls on him for help, he remembers Carla's words and says, "Friend, what you're seeking is found in Christ. Why don't you commit your life to him?"

32

THE "MINI-BIBLE" JESUS

It was a cold snowy day when eight-year-old Mecca Wuellner had what she later called her "first moment with Jesus."

She was standing in Nanny Dora's kitchen, holding a "mini-Bible" in her hands. This children's book contained a quote from each book of the Bible, but Mecca wasn't interested in the quotes this day.

Today, she was transfixed by a picture.

Gazing into her book, Mecca couldn't take her eyes off an etching of Jesus hanging on the cross. His lifeless body hung with his head bowed down. The dark lines drawn diagonally from the sky accented his grief. It seemed as though the sky was sobbing, and Mecca winced in grief that Jesus had to die. It seemed so unfair.

She read more pages of the Bible and looked at more pictures, not knowing what to make of them all, then closed the book and went about the day.

Through the rest of her growing up years, Mecca remembered that day in Nanny Dora's kitchen when she felt sad about Jesus, but her family's strong religious tradition replaced what might have been a growing relationship with Christ himself. She was schooled in a thorough religious system of rules and codes, but her heart missed the personal relationship with Jesus Christ.

The teachers at her religious school taught that devotion to God was the highest calling—but if that were really true, Mecca wondered why the nuns who taught her seemed so burdened. It didn't make sense.

When the time came for Mecca to attend college, she realized her obligation to her religious training could finally be broken. She felt liberated—to party, to indulge in unhealthy relationships, to live a life in which she made the rules. But with each new "freedom" came an intense feeling of emptiness.

At night Mecca would lie awake, crying out to God for forgiveness and direction. One night in 1990, she made a decision to stop crying and seek the truth about life—no matter how long it took.

The following year Mecca moved to another city and was invited by a friend to attend a college-career group at Grace Community Church. *How corny,* she thought as she listened to the singing and clapping of the group. Then Richard, the Bible teacher, stood to speak. Using the Bible as his guide, he spoke about truth, life, and everyday frustrations. Mecca yearned to hear more.

She returned to the group week after week. Richard always spoke about topics that were relevant to her—*and* he went to the Bible for answers. Mecca recalls, "For the first time in my life I believed that God was speaking to me, and he was saying that Jesus Christ was the way, the truth, and the life I was seeking."

For two more years Mecca endured the tension of unhealthy relationships and the wooing of God's Spirit. The pressure of those relationships suffocated her. Something had to change. She decided that if she could escape to Colorado and spend a summer with her parents, she would find relief.

Instead, she found the Colorado summer filled with partying and guy chasing. Then something happened on the night of July 13, 1993.

Mecca lay in her bed reflecting on her life. In the stillness, she felt the loving gentle presence of the Holy Spirit. "Mecca Lee, what are you doing?"

Tears welled up in Mecca's eyes. She choked back a sob. She knew only Jesus could fill her emptiness. He was the Friend she needed to take away the loneliness that consumed her. Completely disclosing her heart to Jesus, Mecca turned her life—her whole being—over to him. She reached for an unused Bible nearby, opened the pages, and realized that she was opening a new chapter of her life as well.

When she returned home at summer's end, she

knew she was a new creature. For the first time in her life, she sensed that she was on her own with the *one true Lord*. Everything seemed new, for her life had been redeemed.

33

PRETTY LITTLE
PIGTAILS

Jonathan Slocumb's infectious brand of comedy has
mesmerized audiences everywhere. Drawing from
the rich heritage of his Christian faith, Jonathan
finds many ways to spark a laugh. Sometimes he'll
do it with his crack-up imitations of Martin Luther
King Jr., and James Brown. Other times he'll get a
guffaw by suggesting humorous twists on classic
hymns. (For example, if the churchgoer in the pew
next to you has bad breath, instead of singing
"Amen," try belting out a chorus of "A-Mint!") But
no matter what he's doing, he's always clean and
always good for a laugh.

Even though Jonathan's stand-up material is
obviously based on Christianity, he's been accepted
in both gospel and mainstream circles. He has
opened for The Winans, Take 6, Kirk Franklin,
Aretha Franklin, Natalie Cole, and Toni Braxton.
He has performed on the *700 Club* and *Def*

Comedy Jam and has played Clyde the Slide in the WB Network sitcom *The Steve Harvey Show*.

Ask this comedian what keeps him going without slipping into the norm of raunchy jokes and foul language, and he'll point back to when he was ten years old, when his great-aunt made an announcement to her young relative: "I'm going to take you out to the tent tomorrow night."

To this ten-year-old, a tent meant one thing: Ringling Brothers' Barnum and Bailey Circus! But that wasn't the tent his aunt meant. She meant that they were going to a tent revival meeting. So the next night Jonathan and his aunt went to the tent.

Jonathan was immediately disappointed. He had expected to see elephants and clowns and acrobats. Instead, he saw a bunch of old people standing around singing "There shall be showers of blessing . . ."

This ain't no tent! Jonathan thought to himself. Disgusted, he turned to his left—and saw a vision!

The vision was Frances Scurry. Eleven years old with pretty little pigtails and a smiling face, Frances inspired only one thought in Jonathan: *Whoooo!*

This young Romeo had seen enough. He didn't really care about all the singing and preaching, but if Frances Scurry was going to the tent meetings, Jonathan was going to go too. So, tagging along with his great-aunt, Jonathan went to church at night in hopes of seeing the pretty girl.

But bit by bit the message in those meetings began to sink in to Jonathan's head, and the Holy Spirit began to convict him. When the revival was over, Jonathan's family joined a Seventh-Day

Adventist church nearby. Through the revival services he came to understand that Christianity meant giving all of himself—every thought, attitude, and action—to Jesus and receiving Jesus' forgiveness for all the things he'd done wrong. Then he prayed to God, asking him to take over his life and to forgive him for the wrongs he'd done.

Now, many years later, that initial commitment has stayed with the man who combines the holy with the hilarious. And God used Frances Scurry's pretty little pigtails to begin this work of transformation.

34

AFTER THE FALL

As she slowly regained consciousness, Janice Huey heard her mother reading from the devotional book *Hind's Feet on High Places*. Blurry forms took shape as her eyes struggled to focus. She reached up to touch her lovely brown hair, but it was gone, replaced with a gauze cap covering her head.

Then the memories flooded back and the pieces fell together. Janice's friend Kathy had invited her to go on a twenty-one-day rafting trip on the Colorado River down into the Grand Canyon. Janice happily joined Kathy's friends from Idaho State University for this adventure. The wild ride down the river was exhilarating, the company entertaining. Janice was having the time of her life.

On day nineteen, someone suggested a rock-climbing excursion, and Janice eagerly agreed. After free climbing halfway up the hundred-foot granite wall, she felt her fingers slipping. Terror numbed her mind as her feet slid off their perches. Screaming, Janice lost her grip completely and fell.

She tumbled forty feet down the rock, landing on her head at the bottom. At first, many of her new friends feared she had died, but by God's grace, she was still alive. An air-evacuation helicopter rushed Janice, who had severe head injuries and a fractured neck, from the bottom of the Grand Canyon to a hospital in Phoenix.

Now Janice was lying in a hospital bed, wondering why she was still alive. Recovery was painful and depressing, but she experienced an awareness of God. Loving friends surrounded her, prayed for her, and cheered for her. She progressed remarkably. Within two weeks she was able to walk a mile and a half under her own power! The doctors released her to return to her parents' home in southern California.

At home she relived her injury many times. She began to realize how she lived her life dangling on the thread of rebellion—no time for God, little interest in following Jesus. The climbing injury brought Janice face-to-face with her rebellion. The near-death experience had softened her heart, making her open to receive God's profound love.

Hunched over from back and neck pain and wearing a scarf to cover her bald head, Janice felt God extending his love to her through others. John and Jay took her to their volleyball games. Gina and Jeanette called or walked with her. Craig, an assistant pastor, provided transportation for church activities. And Wayne—crazy Wayne—made her laugh with all his antics.

On July 11 Janice went to a Christian rock concert at Calvary Chapel in Costa Mesa, California. She was surprised to hear contemporary music with a message that spoke of Jesus and his love for her! She testifies, "I heard how he could take my sins that burdened me and give me new life."

Janice desperately wanted that new life. When an opportunity came at the end of the concert, she got up from her seat and went to the front of the auditorium. Broken physically and spiritually, she bowed her head and asked Jesus to forgive her rebellious streak, to come in and live in her forever. God's hands had caught Janice, even after the fall. She lives now with gratitude for each day. "My life has never been the same. I've known his peace, joy, and love for many years."

35

FROM THE LAKE OF FIRE TO
THE LOVE OF CHRIST

The speaker was emphatic. "The Bible says that all liars will be cast into the lake of fire!" he shouted.

The girl on the first row was squirming. She thought the front would be an ideal place to sit, and the enthusiastic singing had inspired her. But this dynamic speaker was getting too personal. Nancy's mind flashed back to the incident that happened earlier in the week. She had lied to her mother, and she could feel the fear creeping up the back of her neck.

This was Nancy Little's first experience of Youthtime, Buffalo's local high school youth rally. Youthtime was a weekly Christian meeting filled with excitement, games, songs, and fun. Nancy had wanted to come for months, but her older brother didn't want his kid sister tagging along. It appeared that she would never get to go.

Nancy was a freshman at North Tonawanda

High School. During one of her homeroom periods she told a new friend, Valine, about this exciting event called Youthtime. "Boy, I'd love to go some Saturday night."

To her surprise Valine knew what she was talking about. "What a coincidence! I go every Saturday. Why don't you go with me? I hitch a ride with an older couple, Mr. and Mrs. Reynolds, and I know they'd be happy for you to go too."

Nancy could hardly contain her excitement. The following Saturday Nancy went to Youthtime and sat on the front row! But when the speaker began talking about hellish lakes of fire, Nancy felt uncomfortable. She knew she was a sinner, and she felt troubled about it.

Fortunately the speaker went on to tell how the Lord had made a way for sin to be forgiven. God had allowed his Son, Jesus Christ, to take the punishment for Nancy's sin. All she needed to do was to receive this gracious gift.

Though Nancy left the auditorium that night troubled by her sin, she also felt hopeful that a way of escape was available. So the next Saturday night she went to Youthtime, again sat on the front row, and found herself looking into the face of another speaker. He also spoke of God's amazing love for sinners and invited those who would like to trust Christ to come forward to receive counsel.

Nancy's heart said, "Move," but her feet wouldn't cooperate. She was too afraid.

Later that week she told Valine how she longed to become a child of God through Christ. She felt regret for not praying with someone at Youthtime. Valine's face lit up.

"Nancy, I'll walk forward with you next Saturday night. I'd be glad to." When Saturday night rolled around, Nancy wasted no time. With Valine at her side, she boldly moved to the front of the auditorium. There she prayed, asking God to forgive her sins; she confessed that Christ endured death for her sake so she would not have to.

Today Nancy Little lives in Cambridge, Ontario. Recently she was watching a television program. On stage was a large portrait of a famous personality. But a closer look revealed that the picture was actually a composite of tiny portraits of thousands of people. She realized that this was a beautiful example of how she had been drawn into the love of Christ. She felt a profound sense of gratitude as she reflected back on those life-changing events.

"It has been many years since I became a Christian, but I still see the faces of those faithful people who cared about the state of my soul—my brother, Valine, the Reynoldses, the Youthtime staff, and those preachers. My coming to the Lord is a composite picture of those faithful Christians linked in God's beautiful plan to form the picture of a young girl with the joy of the Lord on her face."

36

DON'T LOOK AWAY

Christian musician John Cox still doesn't know
her name, but he'll always remember the young
woman who interrupted his 1995 concert in
Dallas. She was just another face in the crowd until
she stood up and began walking toward the stage.

John was telling a story, making his way through
an elaborate introduction of the next song.
Suddenly the woman was in front of him, one arm
outstretched in John's direction. John wasn't sure
how to react at first. Then he noticed the woman
was holding something—a napkin. For some reason
she was trying to hand that napkin to him.

He reached for it, and without a word she
returned to her seat for the rest of the concert.
John glanced down at the paper in his hand.

"Play the song 'Don't Look Away.'"

He looked again. *Yep, just a song request.* But
there was something else.

John nearly forgot he was on stage as he read the story the woman had scribbled on the napkin. . . .

She sat, tired and spent, in the car, waiting in the parking lot. The needle tracks that dotted her arms revealed a deadly dependence, an addiction that would either kill her or leave her constantly craving more of the substance that wreaked havoc with her mind and body.

The year was 1992, and at that moment she wanted to just sit and listen. The tape, a gift from a friend, played on her car stereo. A rough-voiced singer and his gritty guitar spoke to her. She turned up the volume. The song was a simple tune called "Don't Look Away." The artist, John Cox, sang with a passion she could almost touch. He told her that she needed God.

"Every time I look around," he sang, "I start to sink and I'm swallowed by the sea." She caught her breath. *That's me!* she thought, listening harder now, hanging on every word.

The chorus came around. "I hear Jesus say he can't hurt you now/Don't look away, just keep your eyes on me. . . ."

There was something about that song . . . no, there was something about the Person John was singing about. Suddenly she craved that Person more than any drug, more than anything. She could sense that he craved her too, like a father longing for his daughter to come home.

Right at that moment, alone in her car, she called out to Jesus, begging him to save her. And right at that moment, joining her in that car, Jesus did. Never again would drugs control her life. She was God's daughter, and she had come home.

Three years later she heard that John Cox was coming to town for a concert; she had to go. At the concert she could barely control her excitement. This talented singer had such a passion for Jesus, and God had used that passion to bring the young woman to himself. But the singer didn't know about it. Almost without thinking, she grabbed a napkin and scribbled her story on it. She couldn't wait—she had to give it to him now.

When John finished reading the napkin, he wept compassionately. Then he remembered where he was, settled his guitar, and looked over the audience. "There's no way I can explain this to you now, so I'm just going to go on to the next song." And he sang "Don't Look Away."

John looks back on that night. "That song provided a highway for her to see God directly in front of her. As a musician, that's your highest calling right there. That just totally blew me away—and it still does. I've still got the napkin."

37

"I CAN HEAL MYSELF!"

I don't need doctors. And I don't need God either! I can heal myself, Phil Lockard liked to brag to himself. He even believed what he said.

But it was becoming increasingly obvious that what he believed wasn't working. Phil's internal pain was becoming unbearable, and frequent bleeding from bladder tumors reminded him that his determination wasn't healing him. Something had to be done.

This rancher's I-can-do-it-myself attitude was crumbling. All his life his pride had led the way. The excruciating pain he was in forced him to admit he needed medical help. Reluctantly he made an appointment at the Veterans Hospital in the area. He thought they'd give him some medicine and send him home. In fact, Phil was heading out the door of the hospital when an intern rushed up to him.

"Don't leave! I've just received the test results. Your condition is very serious. We're admitting you to the intensive care unit right away." Within an hour, Mr. Self-Sufficient found himself lying in bed with a needle in his arm receiving a blood transfusion. He was not a happy man.

At that point Phil noticed another drama reaching a climax in the bed next to him. The man in the other bed was moaning, yelling, screaming. The curtain that separated the two men couldn't mask the trauma. Suddenly a "code red" was called, and medical personnel rushed into Phil's room. Frantically they tried to resuscitate the dying man. *Whump. Whump. Whump.* The sound of the electrical charges coursing through his roommate's body blasted in Phil's ears.

Then silence.

The man had exited ignominiously into eternity.

Phil had never even seen the man before, yet the death scene played over and over again in his mind. *What if that had been me?* He was deeply troubled.

While he cogitated, a nurse with some free time entered the room and started a conversation with him. She was from the Philippines, and she told him about her past life, the problems she had encountered, and how she had placed her faith in Jesus Christ. "Mr. Lockard, why don't you let Jesus Christ come into your life so you can find the joy I've discovered?"

Phil considered it. He felt troubled by the recent events, but his stubbornness remained. Phil stayed in the hospital another week until the medical treatment took hold. Then he was allowed to return to his ranch. The medicine seemed to be healing his body, yet a gnawing emptiness consumed his soul. He thought moving to a new city would help.

While he was alone in a strange city, Phil finally admitted to himself that he needed spiritual help. He went to a Bible study where a wise godly teacher opened the Word of God and spoke of God's great love in Jesus Christ. Phil knew this was what he needed.

One morning Phil and two of his Bible study friends were talking and eating breakfast together. One of the men talked about the power and forgiveness to be found in Jesus. The Holy Spirit softened Phil's heart, and his barriers of pride crumbled. There in the restaurant Phil Lockard finally bowed his head and surrendered the control of his life to Jesus Christ.

He can now attest to God's patience. "For the first time I knew that I was home. You know that nurse at the hospital? Well, I've gone back to the hospital several times, and no one remembers her working there. She seems to have been there just for me. It makes you wonder, doesn't it?"

38

LARRY'S KITCHEN

It wasn't Larry Norman's Christianity that made seventeen-year-old Randy Stonehill want to get to know him better; it was Larry's music. To Randy, music was a religion in itself. Music captivated and inspired him. He loved the music of his old guitar and his handwritten lyrics.

When Randy found out that Larry was also a musician, it felt natural to get together and talk. But somehow the conversation in the kitchen strayed from the norm. Instead of guitars and albums and the latest equipment in music stores, Larry and Randy started talking about God.

God was the last thing on Randy's mind. Having just moved out on his own, this California kid was thinking about making the transition from boyhood to manhood. He was thinking about survival and success in the world of adults. But there was something about Larry's questions that

Randy couldn't dodge—these questions about life, God, the heart, the soul, and heaven, hell, peace, and eternity.

Randy says now, "God just breathed on that [conversation] so that those questions rang in the core of my being."

One day Larry asked the unavoidable question. "Do you want to pray right now and accept Jesus Christ into your life?"

In his mind and heart, Randy knew the answer was yes. Nearly thirty years later, he remembers that moment with vivid clarity.

"It was an incredible surprise. I could only describe it as otherworldly, which is appropriate because all of a sudden my world was invaded and my reality was turned upside down forever.

"I just remember praying and then leaning up against this guy's wall with my eyes shut and exhaling. And as I exhaled, it was like a physical burden left me, some kind of darkness or something. And I actually felt lighter and taller. I felt incredibly naked and frightened. But the overriding feeling that made it all OK was I felt incredibly loved."

Randy Stonehill continued making music, only this time he made music for Christ. He and Larry blazed a trail many years ago that has helped many other Christians since then to create Jesus-focused music.

39

THE ETERNAL
ROMANCE

Live radio is supposed to be easy, but for Christian romance novelist Robin Jones Gunn, the interview on the local station suddenly became an uncomfortable experience.

Though no one could see him, the interviewer pointed his finger directly at Robin and spoke accusingly over the air. "How can you call yourself a Christian and support the romance industry by writing romance novels?"

Robin took a deep breath. "When I was a teen, I read a love story that changed my life. It was the story of a relentless lover who would never give up on his first love. In the first few chapters everything falls apart. Three-fourths of the way through the book, he does everything he can to prove his love for her and still she won't come back to him. Then finally, in the last chapter, he comes riding in on a white horse and takes her away to be his bride and live with him forever."

The interviewer smirked and retorted for his audience, "Sounds like a cheesy formula-romance paperback. How did that change your life?"

"Formula romance? Cheesy paperback? I was talking about the Bible. White horse and everything. God is the relentless lover, and he will never stop pursuing us, because we are his first love."

Robin's strange response silenced the interviewer. Abruptly he cut to a commercial, and Robin pondered her first meeting with God, the relentless lover. . . .

Twelve-year-old Robin Jones was listening to the speaker. Having grown up in church, she had learned much about Jesus but did not yet know him one-on-one. That's where summer camp and the camp speaker came in. The speaker's words impressed her. "God doesn't have any grandchildren. Just because your parents are Christians, that doesn't make you a Christian. You must become his child by receiving Jesus Christ."

The message stirring within her, Robin knew she wanted to know this Jesus for herself. At the time of decision Robin eagerly rushed forward to find her camp counselor. She wanted to pray for Jesus to come into her life to make her his child, and she wanted a counselor to help her know what to say. Her cabin mate, Kath, also prayed to receive Jesus.

Of this experience, Robin says, "I remember

feeling fresh that night, after having a good cry back at the cabin. Fresh, and very deeply committed."

Since then, Robin has written romance novels that get to the heart of being a child of God. Her books have been read by women in other parts of the world. In her files at home, Robin has a stack of letters from women in Africa—all young ladies who have read her romance stories and been affected by them.

One letter in that stack is special. A girl in Zimbabwe wrote Robin to ask how she could become a Christian like the characters in Robin's books. She, too, wanted to meet that relentless Lover, and Robin was happy to introduce her to God.

40

IN THE BOOK?

"If anyone's name was not found written in the book of life, he was thrown into the lake of fire" (Revelation 20:15, NIV).

The words attached themselves to Virgie's mind. The "book of life," as described in the biblical book of Revelation, refers to a list God keeps of people who will live eternally with him. Turning from the Bible, she gazed out the window as a silent prayer formulated. *God, how can my name be written in the book of life? I want to go to heaven when I die.*

Virgie grew up in the Philippines, and her first exposure to the Bible had come through a high school literature class. Her teacher introduced the class to the book of Psalms. Virgie read some from Genesis, then grew impatient and decided she wanted to know what happened at the end. Flipping through the pages of the Bible, she paused near the end of the book of Revelation; there she read about the book of life. That one verse dominated her thoughts.

Following high school Virgie enrolled in college. During her freshman year, an American missionary from Campus Crusade shared the "Four Spiritual Laws" with a group of students: God has a good plan for our lives; we are separated from God by sin; Jesus Christ is the only remedy for this problem of separation; and we must repent of our sin and humbly receive Christ in order to know God. "I must admit that it went in one ear and out the other," says Virgie. Nevertheless, she decided to go to a Bible study.

One day in the Bible study a fellow student used the analogy of a chasm between God and man: "Jesus Christ is the bridge by which we can come to the Lord." Virgie knew she was separated from God, but she just didn't feel prompted to act.

I'm searching, she decided. She attended an extracurricular class in transcendental meditation.

One night to escape boredom, Virgie clicked on the television and flipped through the channels, looking for entertainment. One show quickly grabbed her attention. An energetic preacher was talking about God! (She found out later it was Billy Graham.) He said that a person could have a "personal relationship with Jesus Christ."

I've always known about Jesus, but I didn't know that he wanted to know me personally, she thought. The preacher said Jesus was like a bridge we could use to get to God. Somehow it all began to make sense.

At the close of the broadcast the evangelist invited his listeners to enter into that personal relationship. Bowing her head in front of the TV set, Virgie Lloyd prayed, asking Jesus to enter her life and to be her "bridge" into a lasting, intimate relationship with God. When she finished praying, she knew she had found the way to God and that Jesus had now written her name in the "book of life."

"It had to take three times for me to hear the gospel before I could understand it. But I'm sure glad I understand it now."

41

THE CALLING

It was late, and Carmen was tired, but she *had* to know. Carmen Hilton had to know if God was real and, if he was, whether or not he was strong enough to break the chains of darkness that shackled her life.

Clutching a Christian tract, Carmen read a "sinner's prayer" she'd found in the back, a prayer asking Jesus to forgive her sins and come into her life. She hoped it was true, prayed it was true. But Carmen wasn't sure if God would want her—a daughter of a witch and a practicing medium as well. After all, wasn't that her calling?

Her mother had different plans altogether for little Carmen. Carmen's mother was a practicing witch and spiritualist; during a séance she had dedicated her daughter to a life of spiritualism. Carmen was only eight years old then.

As she grew up in the New York City area

called Spanish Harlem, Carmen became more heavily involved in spiritualism. With her mother as a partner, she would regularly hold séances and tell fortunes to hundreds of clamoring customers.

In her heart, however, Carmen struggled. She longed for God. "But spiritualism *is* following God," others protested. "You're following God through spiritualism."

Can this really be of God? she thought. Deep inside, her heart responded with a loud, persistent "No!"

Still, she followed in the "family business," moving further and further into the world of spirits, séances, fortune-telling, and witchery. With every new step she plunged deeper and deeper into depression. Mental anguish regularly overcame her as she desperately looked for a way out of her supposed "calling."

At that time another girl—a Christian—befriended Carmen. "Carmen," she'd say, "that's NOT the way to go!"

Finally Carmen agreed to join her friend in attending a service at a small Pentecostal church. Carmen sat in church and listened, really listened. And for the first time in years, Carmen felt the darkness of her life lifting; she felt hope and new courage. She knew Jesus *had* to be the way she was so desperately seeking.

At home that night, still gripping the tract she'd gotten at the church, Carmen read along with the prayer of forgiveness. She added, "God, if you're real and what I have is not real, I have to feel something different. I have to feel you come into my life."

At that moment, "I literally felt what I know was his blood cleansing me, and I felt the chains of darkness broken." She had found the way. She was free at last.

Carmen's brother soon invited her to join him in attending services at the Brooklyn Tabernacle church. On New Year's Eve she walked into the building and was stunned by the reality of God's presence. She broke down and cried with joy. "It was like a dam burst! I felt cleansed."

A few months later, Carmen tried out for the Brooklyn Tabernacle choir and made it. If you've seen the Brooklyn Tabernacle choir on television recently, chances are you've seen Carmen Hilton singing and praising God. Her smiling face and harmonious notes reveal a person who has found the Prince of Peace, Jesus Christ, and has allowed his Spirit alone to rule her life.

42

TIME RUNNING OUT?

"Scott, I dreamed about you last night," the girl said in math class. At fifteen Scott liked to imagine that all girls were dreaming about him. What puzzled him about this girl's confession was that this was only his second day at this new school, and she had been absent the day before. The girl continued, explaining that in her dream God had made it clear that she was to meet this new student so that he could learn about God.

In his most polite voice Scott informed her that he was not a Christian. Since the third grade he'd known that Jesus Christ had died on the cross for his sins. He just didn't want to be a Christian. Scott's indifference only challenged his schoolmate more. She determined to become his friend. And, well, she *was* cute. So Scott decided that hanging out with her wouldn't be a totally bad idea, even if she was into Jesus.

A couple of weeks later the girl laid a Bible in Scott's hands. "I bought this for you and want you to start reading it."

A day or so later, the phone rang. It was Scott's new friend. "Have you read your Bible yet?"

"No," Scott said reluctantly. At that, the girl promptly assigned a Scripture passage for the day and hung up. Thirty minutes later the phone rang. "What did you learn from your reading?"

"What could I do but read the assigned passage?" says Scott. "She just wouldn't let up, so I gave in and began to read the chapters and verses she gave me."

About the same time she was pushing Scott into the Bible, his parents discovered a church they liked. The whole family started attending.

Soon Scott was also attending the Wednesday night youth group. One Wednesday Ross Bennett showed up to teach the Bible in the youth pastor's place. Ross, like the girl in school, took a personal interest in Scott's relationship with Jesus Christ. He asked, "Scott, if you were to die today, would you go to heaven? And tell me why."

Scott could only admit that he would *not* enter heaven. The two of them talked for over an hour, but Scott felt no motivation to change.

The following Sunday as the pastor preached, he reminded his listeners that the Spirit of God only prompts one so many times before he leaves the person alone. Scott found that thought recurring in his mind for the next couple of days. Then came Tuesday afternoon.

Scott was listening to a tape by the heavy metal

band Mötley Crüe. Scott admits, "Oddly enough, this was a tape I had stolen! The words of one song were, 'Hey you, whatta you gonna do when time runs out on you? You better use it before you lose it.'"

The Holy Spirit used those words to finally penetrate Scott's heart. He turned off the tape, bowed his head, and invited Jesus Christ to take control of his life. In a miracle of irony God used a determined schoolgirl and a band known for its godlessness to bring Scott to the doorstep of heaven.

43

PLAYING CHURCH

As a twelve-year-old, Shirley Caesar loved to play, and she loved to sing. It was no accident that these two activities came together in Shirley's backyard. Regulars at the revival meetings at their church, Shirley and her siblings were familiar with the elements of a worship service. So the children were having a grand old time "playing church" in the backyard one Tuesday afternoon.

Mimicking what she had seen at the revival services, Shirley was jumping, dancing, and singing. But as Shirley says, "There's so much power in the name of Jesus, you can only 'play' so much."

Unexpectedly, in the midst of that playing, Shirley got a glimpse of why those adults in the revival were acting the way they did. "I was out there jumping and dancing, and the presence of the Lord just took over. Before I knew it, I'd gone from 'playing' church to really *having* church! A sense of repentance fell on me that I can hardly express."

That night at the revival meeting, Shirley wasted no time. "I didn't even give them time to make the altar call. I made my own altar call, [and] that night I gave my life to the Lord."

Giving her life to Lord meant serving him with her singing as well, even when she felt less than perfect. One day she became ill just before a radio concert in Birmingham, but she was determined to perform. Praying for God's mercy and mustering all her strength, she sang on that live radio show.

God has worked through Shirley since she was a child. She has recorded thirty albums and won many Stellar and Dove awards. Her voice and message are recognized in both gospel and mainstream circles. This long ministry has opened the hearts of millions to the love of God, who intervened when a little girl was *playing* church and transformed her into *a part of* the church instead.

44

WIFE QUEST

I'd like to get married, Steve Behlke mused to himself. *After all, it's about time for me to settle down. Only trouble is, none of the girls I've been dating is the kind of woman I'd want to marry.*

Though Steve had attended church regularly as a child, he quit when he was a teenager. The party life was too attractive. By the time he entered his twenties he was accustomed to the three *p*s: pot, parties, and pretty girls.

In spite of who he'd become, Steve wanted to spend his life with someone better.

I want to marry a . . . godly woman. I guess the place I'd find a woman like that is in church.

Steve went to the only church he felt comfortable in—the church he'd known in his childhood. Steve was immediately disappointed. The church's congregation was filled with older adults. No pretty young girls in sight!

But he kept coming back. The return to church caused him to think about both Jesus Christ and the emptiness of his own life. Unfortunately, the pastor's sermons did not satisfy Steve's spiritual hunger. He decided he'd have to find help elsewhere.

One day in a phone conversation with his father, Steve mentioned that he was going to church again. A few days later he received a package in the mail from his dad that contained Josh McDowell's book *Evidence That Demands a Verdict*.

Steve dug into it voraciously. The more he read, the more the book provoked a desire to read the Bible. His dad encouraged him to read the Old Testament, while his older sister—who had become a Christian a few years earlier—pointed him to the Gospel of John.

A process of growth and understanding began to take place in Steve's life. In the weeks that followed he had conversations about the Lord on the phone with his sister and father. He continued reading the Bible and made new discoveries as he read *Evidence That Demands a Verdict*. More and more his mind was becoming satisfied with the truth he encountered there.

Then one night as he was finishing McDowell's book, Steve became aware of a new reality. Here's how he describes that moment:

"I knew what was true, and I realized that I could confidently trust that Jesus Christ had died for my sins. And I knew that he had risen from the dead exactly like he said he would. That night I was born again. I was cleansed. I was reconciled with my heavenly Father." In the days following this experience Steve often strolled along the beach late at night enjoying this new real relationship with Jesus Christ. This closeness has grown even more precious over the years.

Steve's interest in Christianity began when he decided to seek a godly wife. During Steve's journey Polly, a friend from days past, was checking out books at the library where Steve's mom worked. His mother gave Steve's phone number to Polly. A phone call renewed the friendship, which culminated a year later in marriage—to just the type of godly woman Steve had envisioned.

45

HAPPILY EVER
AFTER

December 1978. A nervous twenty-year-old groom and his nineteen-year-old bride stood before their pastor. They had just finished exchanging vows.

"I now pronounce you husband and wife," the minister said. Jeff and Mary Bauer prepared to ride off into the golden sunset and live happily ever after. Both had been reared in sound moral homes. They loved each other and were excited about their future.

But a silent enemy was lurking quietly nearby, waiting to drive a wedge into the marriage relationship and destroy Jeff's life. Alcoholism was slowly gaining a stranglehold on him.

The scene shifts to August 1980. Jeff and Mary have welcomed little Jill into the family. In May of 1982 Kristin is born. But as the family grew, the marriage suffered. And the grip of alcohol tightened.

In July of 1985, the problem is exposed when Jeff is arrested on a DWI (Driving While Intoxicated) offense. He entered an outpatient program for alcoholics but continued to live in denial. "Though I remained sober for twenty months, I was really a 'dry drunk.'"

Jeff's alcoholism continued to suck the life out of his marriage. In November of 1987 Jeff and Mary separated for the third time—for seven months. During these months of loneliness Jeff began to reevaluate his life. The process led him to a new insight. He realized that he had tried to do what Mary and others thought would better his life. At this juncture he saw the barrenness of his own soul and knew he needed to help himself.

"During that separation I finally hit an emotional bottom. I knew that my life was really out of my control, and I desperately needed God's help."

Mary's sister, Patty, had become a Christian. Jeff observed her joy and purpose for living, but he quietly mocked her. Now he was open to the possibility that God might be the answer to his need. So he picked up the phone and called her for counsel.

"Jeff, you need to see a pastor. You need spiritual help."

He went to the last church he had attended and made an appointment to see a pastor there. "You need to start praying," said the pastor.

"But I don't know how to pray. What do I say? How do I begin?"

"You learn by doing it. It'll seem awkward at

the beginning but will become more natural as you progress. Just do it!"

So Jeff prayed.

During the separation Mary had started attending the church that her neighbors attended. Mary and Jeff came back together and sought counseling from the pastor there, a gifted man who helped individuals find healing. He helped Jeff learn that God loved him. They began attending that church together. Jeff listened to the pastor preach from the Bible every week, and he began to understand the Good News of Jesus' death on the cross in a new meaningful way.

"When I attended Alcoholics Anonymous I regularly heard about relying on a 'higher power.' I didn't dispute God's existence, but I didn't understand what a relationship with God was about."

But now in this church it was beginning to make sense. Soon the day came when Jeff bowed his head and accepted God's gift of eternal life. Both husband and wife were baptized as a testimony of their newfound faith in Christ.

Jeff and Mary began to reconstruct their marriage, even renewing their wedding vows to each other. With the presence of Christ in their home they found a solid foundation that gave them strength and purpose. Now Jeff and Mary both look forward to another kind of "happily ever after"—the one that's guaranteed for eternity.

46

MOUNTAIN-MOVING
FAITH

Chris Evans was at Debbie's apartment when she saw it. Lying on the bed in front of God and everybody was a Bible, opened to the book of Matthew.

As she scanned the text, Chris was drawn to the words of Matthew 17:20. " 'You didn't have enough faith,' Jesus told them. 'I assure you, even if you had faith as small as a mustard seed you could say to this mountain, "Move from here to there," and it would move. Nothing would be impossible.' "

That can't be true, Chris thought. She turned to her friend. "What does this verse mean?" Though Debbie's answer didn't make that much sense to Chris, the verse made her realize that she didn't have that kind of faith—the kind that could actually move mountains.

A gnawing hunger to search out the reality of

that faith was planted in Chris's heart that day. Her religious upbringing left this teenager with only a set of rules, not a mountain-moving faith capable of anything. She actively participated in the unwholesome parties of her friends, acting out her rebellion in destructive behaviors toward herself and others. That, in turn, left Chris feeling guilty and full of regrets. Still, every time she tried to "clean up her act," she inevitably lapsed into apathy, which led to a vicious cycle of partying, guilt, repentance, apathy; partying, guilt, repentance, apathy. . . .

Then Debbie invited Chris to go to a youth camp with other young adults from her church. There they would be gathering for fun and biblical instruction. "I'll get back to you," Chris replied. *That's an odd thing to do. Why would anyone want to go to a religious camp to have fun?*

The first night at camp, Chris felt confused. She was curious about what kind of people would come to a place like this. Her main concern was, *Is this going to be fun?*

The next morning she headed into the woods for a relaxing walk. Debbie stopped her and encouraged her to come to a meeting where Jim Brock, the head coach of the Arizona State University baseball team, was to speak. Chris assented.

Jim's words targeted Chris's heart. "God doesn't want you to try to clean up your act so you can come to him. He invites you to come to him and let him make the changes."

No one needed to convince Chris that she was

a sinner. She thought of those parties she'd been attending, the rebellious streak that so irritated her parents, the bad choices she'd made, and the consequences she was experiencing.

A ray of hope broke through as Jim's words continued to penetrate Chris's heart. "Jesus Christ has already died for all the sins you've committed. Why not accept his forgiveness and the new everlasting life he is waiting to give you?"

When Jim invited others to pray a prayer after him, Chris resonated with the words. "As I prayed, I felt a ton of weight being lifted off my shoulders. The guilt of all my sinful actions vanished. Suddenly the difference between knowing *about* Jesus and *knowing* Jesus became crystal clear. I left that room excited about this new relationship with him. And in the days that followed, the hunger to know him was endless."

Twenty years later, Chris Evans finds great joy in teaching other women about the one who loves them unconditionally. Her hunger to intimately know him continues to draw her to him. The discoveries are still fresh and fulfilling. "When I stopped trying to 'clean up my act' and ran to him when I failed, that's when I discovered the gracious, loving friend that Jesus is."

47

MUHAMMAD OR
JESUS?

"There is only one God, and Muhammad is his prophet." The words of her grandfather rang in Zahea (pronounced "Zuh-HAY-ya") Hassen's ears as she paged her way through a Bible given to her by a friend. "That is what the Islamic Druse religion believes. You were born a Druse, Zahea, and you will always be a Druse."

Growing up as a child of Lebanese immigrants to America, Zahea knew she was supposed to be a Druse, but something inside her balked at that idea. She hungered for God and for truth.

Why are there so many religions? she questioned. *Are they all right? Which religion is true?*

This gifted high school student decided to find out, launching her own personal study of the world's major religions. Long ago she had come to the conclusion that there must be one and only one absolutely correct manner in which to be reconciled to God. She was determined to find that way, to find the truth.

She turned another page in the Bible and read about Jesus, about how he came to earth to reconcile people to God, paid the penalty for sin through his execution on a cross, and defeated death once and for all by rising from the dead.

Was this the truth? She had to find out. Turning to a friend, a pastor in her hometown, Zahea begged to hear more. Reverend Frank Baugh fascinated this seventeen-year-old with his answers to her questions and his stories of Jesus. Her hunger grew.

At that point Zahea began to read the Bible without stopping. Two Scriptures leaped from the pages and planted themselves in her heart: John 3:16, which read in her old English version of the Bible, "For God so loved the world, that he gave his only begotten Son, that whosoever believeth in him should not perish, but have everlasting life" (KJV); and Acts 16:31, "Believe on the Lord Jesus Christ, and thou shalt be saved, and thy house" (KJV).

Zahea was torn. Here was the truth: Jesus—not Muhammad, Islam, or the Koran—is the true way to God. Yet she remembered the words of her grandfather. "You were born a Druse, Zahea, and you will always be a Druse."

The pressure of a choice dismayed her. How could she, a mere teenager, reject the religion of her ancestors in favor of Christianity?

Maybe I can be a "closet Christian," Zahea thought one night. *Maybe I can believe in Jesus*

inside, but follow Islam's ways outside. At that
moment another Scripture came to her mind from
the book of Joshua. "Choose you this day whom
ye will serve . . . but as for me and my house, we
will serve the Lord" (Joshua 24:15, KJV).

She was caught. The Scripture "seared both my
brain and my heart. Obediently I knelt down,
repented, confessed my sins, and accepted Jesus
Christ into my heart." Risking family reprisal, she
openly acknowledged her faith in Christ, telling
anyone who would listen that Jesus is the only way
to God.

But Zahea's family did not renounce their
Christian daughter. Many family members even
listened to her testimony. Years later, Zahea was
instrumental in leading many members of her
family and her own children into a relationship
with Jesus.

Her children are grateful—especially one.
Inheriting his mother's married name of Nappa,
it's he who tells you this story and the stories of
others in this book.

48

CANDY STORE EVANGELIST
(NORM'S STORY)

As a shy twelve-year-old boy, I slipped into my favorite candy store for one of my regular visits. Miss Taylor, a cheerful, gray-haired lady, stood behind the counter. I liked her a lot. She had taken an interest in me and chatted with me about things I thought interesting.

Today I had a razor-sharp appetite for some chocolate-covered cream drops. I eyed them as though I hadn't eaten for a week. So Miss Taylor scooped out several and weighed them on the scales. As she worked, she asked me a question.

"Norm, I've been wondering. Does your family attend any church?"

"No. We never go to church."

"Do you think your mom and dad would mind if I asked my pastor to visit your home? I think you might like my church."

"No, I'm sure they wouldn't mind." I headed for the door, munching on my candy.

In a few days Pastor Banta paid a visit to the Wakefield household and invited my whole family to the services at Grace Baptist Church. The rest of the family visited only a time or two, but I continued and became a regular member of a Sunday school class taught by Mr. Rice, a young man in his late twenties. I became one of a half dozen energetic boys that Mr. Rice held in check each Sunday.

One Sunday Mr. Rice began class on a different subject. "Today I'd like to tell you about heaven." Then he described this fabulous place Jesus is preparing for those who belong to him. It sounded like a place any boy would want to go. And it was especially appealing to me because my teacher described a loving heavenly Father who is kind and gracious—and likes boys. It was so different from the tense unloving home environment I experienced every day. I knew I wanted to live forever with Jesus.

But then Mr. Rice said, "Boys, there's one huge problem. God can't allow sin in heaven. We could never enter into heaven on our own because we are sinners. Do you know what I mean?"

Did I ever know what Mr. Rice meant! I consistently felt shame and embarrassment over the things I did. It was obvious that I'd never qualify as a candidate for heaven. But I certainly wanted to go there.

"Boys, I have good news for you. Jesus Christ died on the cross for your sins. He died for you so you could spend eternity in heaven with him. If you'll admit to him that you are a sinner and trust him as your Savior, you can become a child of God." It seemed like he was looking straight at me. "Would you like to pray and receive him as your Savior?"

I nodded eagerly. So Mr. Rice led this insecure twelve-year-old in a prayer that changed my life forever. In the years that have followed, Jesus has faithfully nurtured me to spiritual health and fruitfulness.

On that Sunday morning in 1946 I had no comprehension of how a simple prayer would change my future. Not only did I receive the gift of heaven, but my life on earth has been richer than I could conceive.

All I am has come about because of Jesus, and the journey began when a Christian woman at a candy store asked permission to invite me to church. Praise be to my glorious Lord!

49

NO LONGER A JUDAS
(MIKE'S STORY)

"Judas Iscariot was a pillar of his community. A fine, upstanding, religious man who inspired others with his virtue."

The words my pastor, Bailey Smith, spoke during that July revival shocked me. Judas? Judas Iscariot? Everyone knew that Judas was one of the Bible's bad guys—one of the worst, in fact. It was Judas who betrayed Jesus, his professed Lord and companion for three years. It was Judas who sold out Jesus for a mere thirty pieces of silver—the price of a common slave.

Bailey must've made a mistake, I thought. *Maybe he meant to say Peter or John or somebody else.* But he kept going.

"In fact, Judas was probably the kind of person mothers hoped their children would grow up to be like. Think about it. Out of the thousands of Christ's early followers, Judas was chosen to be part of the inner circle of twelve disciples. And out of those twelve, Judas alone was selected to be in charge of the group's money. He must have had a sterling reputation to warrant that kind of honor."

I swallowed hard, having a tough time believing what I heard. This was my first time at my church's annual Starlight Crusade. Each year the church would rent the high school football stadium and have two weeks of revival services there. Bailey spoke the clincher that struck deep within me.

"But no matter how good Judas looked on the outside," he said with fire in his voice, "inside he was a man filled with sin." He paused and looked over the faces in the stands. "And maybe he was a man just like you are today."

Bailey spoke for another thirty minutes, but I didn't hear what he said. One thought kept running through my mind: *Maybe Judas was a man just like me.*

Admittedly, I wasn't a man yet. I was only sixteen years old. Still, I'd already begun building quite the reputation as a follower of Jesus.

A few years earlier, I had joined my friends in a string of petty crimes—mostly shoplifting, fighting, and general bad behavior. Before long I was arrested for stealing a bicycle from the school (a crime I didn't commit!). That scared me so much that I determined to turn over a new leaf.

I was actually pretty successful at it. I stopped hanging out with troublemaking friends, stopped cussing, and got involved in my mother's church. I became a leader in the church's youth group and had just been elected vice president of my school's

Youth for Christ club. I led Bible studies for my peers regularly and never missed a church service.

Arrogantly, I had smiled to myself. *Yeah, I must look pretty good to God. Look at all I've done for Jesus these past few years. Look at how much better I am than most of the people my age.*

Bailey's words echoed in my mind again. "No matter how good Judas looked on the outside, inside he was a man filled with sin. And maybe he was a man just like you are today."

I was never happier for a church service to be over than I was that night in 1980. I hurried home and tried to forget what I'd heard my pastor say. Still, I had to go back the next night (what would people think if I missed?), and the next night, and the night after that too. I went every night to that crusade, and every night—no matter what the sermon was about—I kept thinking that maybe I was just another Judas, good on the outside, filthy on the inside.

Finally, mercifully, the allotted two weeks for the Starlight Crusade came to an end. No more would I have to struggle with this inner tension! I had made it through.

Or so I thought. The crusade had been so successful, they decided to extend it for another week! I was stuck. I knew I was going to have to work through this problem, and I knew it had to be soon.

On Monday night, July 14, I went home from church angry. I had a royal argument with God.

"I deserve to go to heaven, God! Look at all these good things I've done. Look at what everybody thinks of me. It'll be embarrassing if I have to admit to the world that I've known all *about* you without knowing you myself. Isn't it enough that I've been a good person and involved in church?"

The silence only confirmed what I knew deep inside. It wasn't enough, and it never would be.

I'd had it. "Fine. If that's the way you want it, you can forget it. I don't need you. Tomorrow I'm starting my life all over—without you." And believe it or not, I fell into a deep sound sleep.

Around 2:00 A.M. I woke suddenly in the darkness. I opened my eyes but could barely see my hand in front of my face. Then I realized the true darkness in which my spirit lived, a darkness cloaked with pride and arrogance. The truth hit me: Nothing I could do would be enough to earn God's favor. *Nothing.* My only hope was Jesus, Jesus alone.

Silently, humbly, and broken to the core, I slipped out of my covers and knelt by the bed. "Jesus, you're right. I can't do it. I'm not good enough. Please forgive my pride; please come, please save me. Please."

Suddenly I felt a deep release, a loosening of the darkness, like a candle had been lit in my soul. Peace filled my heart, silencing the turmoil I'd felt only hours before. I quickly went back to sleep. When I woke the next morning, I could only lie in bed and smile. Jesus had saved me, and I knew it. I could feel it in the peace that enveloped me, in the life-giving fire that now burned inside me.

I was no longer a Judas. New life had begun.

50

BEGINNERS

Our friend and fellow author John Duckworth
related a salvation story so eloquently, we thought it
was appropriate to let him tell this last story to you
in his own words. Listen to John as he remembers a
Sunday school class for three-year-olds:

It wasn't *my* idea to see the Light.

It was all my father's doing.

Not that I was an atheist, a skeptic, or devoted
to another faith. It was just that I was three years
old, and the Light was pretty scary.

That well-lit room scared me, anyway. It was
full of bright colors and chattering children, none
of whom I'd seen before. That was reason enough
to run.

So when my father tried to deposit me for the
first time in Mrs. Loeffler's Sunday school class for
beginners at the First Presbyterian Church of
Flushing, New York, I resisted. Towering

strangers tried to coax me toward a little seat in a sea of little seats, but I knew that was no place for me. Whirling, I stumbled blindly toward my father, who was trying in vain to tiptoe from the room. I wrapped my chubby arms around his legs and wailed.

He must have looked helpless, because Mrs. Loeffler herself had to come to his rescue.

"Why don't you stand in the back of the room?" she suggested to him.

So he did, trying to look reassuring as I was led away. Eventually he sat down.

I sat on a much smaller chair, checking and rechecking over my shoulder to make sure he was still there. All around me were the old hands, the preschoolers who knew what was going on. They knew the songs and the motions, and they knew what was about to happen when Mrs. Loeffler carefully placed a set of paper people on her flannel board at the front of the room. It was story time.

Perhaps the Bible story that day was about Zaccheus, the little paper man who slid up the paper tree to see someone named Jesus. Maybe Mrs. Loeffler led the class in singing about the wee little man and showed us how to claw at that sycamore tree and shade our eyes like sea captains so that we could peer over the crowd, the Savior for to see.

But whether it was Zaccheus, David and Goliath, or Noah, it was all new to me. I could have taught the class all about Santa Claus, the intricacies of leaving a plateful of cookies on Christmas Eve, and listening for the sleigh bells and eight tiny reindeer, but Bible stories were *terra incognita.*

I had never seen the Light, not even a glint or a glow.

So when Mrs. Loeffler stage-managed her cutout characters across that flannel board, I watched. I listened, my fears fading for a moment, and wondered.

And in the back of the room, unknown to me or to Mrs. Loeffler or to anyone but God himself, someone else was watching and wondering. It was a dark-haired, thirty-year-old man who sat on a chair because his little boy would not let him leave. It was my father, who, like me, knew all about Santa Claus but nothing of Zaccheus or Moses or Adam and Eve.

He had never seen the Light, not even a spark or a glimmer. To other grown-ups he called himself an agnostic, and he had come to church only to please his wife and because Sunday school might somehow be a good influence on his son.

So there we were, my father and I, both of us beginners. We were locked in a room full of light with no escape, the son trapped by the father and the father by the son.

We had come to the right place.

The following week we came back. Still unwilling to stay without my father, I made sure he found his spot in the back of the room. Mrs. Loeffler arranged her paper people on the flannel board, and again the Light began to shine.

For the next six weeks it shone as Mrs. Loeffler and her flannel-backed figures told the stories my father and I had never heard. Goliath marched across the flannel, taunting the boyish David, who knocked him flat with a stone and the power of a God we had never met. Adam and Eve hid modestly in the paper bushes, freshly formed by the same God, suddenly barred from their garden home by their wrongdoing—and by a paper angel with a flaming sword.

The Light shone on all of us, but its warmth was felt most deeply by the man in the back of the room. It was not supposed to work this way—that a grown man, a man ten times the age of most of us in the class, would watch so intently. But it did, and as it did, something began to happen in that grown-up heart.

It happened most profoundly the week Mrs. Loeffler told the special story, the one about God's love. Something more than paper and flannel was at work as Mrs. Loeffler revealed the amazing news: God had sent his Son, Jesus, to save people. To save everybody who would believe in him— thirty-year-old fathers, three-year-old sons. Jesus had died for us and then come back to life so that we could live forever.

Sin, death, resurrection, heaven—the Light was too bright for a three-year-old, and most of us in the room were mentally squinting. But far in the back a man was beginning to see.

He had started to hear pieces of this special story, first from his wife who had heard it as she'd grown up, and then from some men of the church who had come to visit. But it had never made this much sense before, had never rung true. It had never been this simple: God loving us and showing it, right there on the flannel board. Anyone could see the innocent Jesus letting go of his life on a cross on a hill, being hidden in a gray paper tomb, and coming back to see his friends—a Mary so happy she might cry at any moment—and disciples so wide-eyed they looked as if they might never calm down. Anyone could see that God had offered people a priceless present, and all we had to do was take it. It was all right there if you only looked.

My father did look and saw and began to believe.

It all happened silently, without any of us knowing. Even Mrs. Loeffler couldn't have known that her old, old story was so new to the man in the back of the room. She couldn't know how deeply he was touched by the simple idea that God loved him. She kept telling the story to the rest of us, moving her paper people around, unconsciously choosing her words for just the right group: the beginners of all ages.

During those six weeks my father and I heard many stories, many songs. But when the time came for Dad to leave because I had finally settled down, one story stood out in his memory. It was the story of God's love, of God sending his Son.

Four months later he was ready to act on the message he'd seen that day. He stepped fully into the Light, asking Jesus to be his Savior. He'd learned many things about Christianity during those four months, but none more important than the simple fact that God loved him.

Already my mother had taken a similar step.

One year later, having seen flashes of Light in people like Mrs. Loeffler and Mom and Dad, I would walk down the burgundy carpet of the sanctuary aisle and give my beginner's heart to Jesus too.

Now we were all beginners together.

Not until three years later did Mrs. Loeffler finally learn all that had happened in the back of her Sunday school room. My parents had to tell her the story before we left town—before we drove across the country to my father's first pastorate. The simple story on the flannel board had changed the whole direction of his life and ours.

Nearly forty years have passed since I sat in Muriel Loeffler's class. I still remember the memory verses I learned there, the action songs, the stories of David and Goliath and Zaccheus and Adam and Eve.

But most of all I remember the wonder of seeing the Light for the first time.

I keep losing sight of that wonder now, and when I do, I want to go back. I want to fly back in time to the fall of 1956, to a bright room with tiny chairs lined up at shiny tables, surrounded by cheerful bulletin boards. I want to sing "Deep and Wide" and do the motions and slip my missionary-offering dime through the slot of the church-shaped bank, and hear it go *clunk* in the bottom.

I want to see Mrs. Loeffler again, smiling and readying her envelope of Bible characters for the softly wrinkled background of the flannel board. I want to hear her say, this time to me, "Why don't you stand in the back of the room?"

And then, older now than my father was when he stood there, I want to watch in wonder as the simplest, most essential story ever told unfolds before my widened eyes. I want to see God loving me, sending his Son to pay for my sins on a hill, bringing him back to a surprising and happy life for me, for me.

I want to see the light, just the Light, for itself. For himself.

I want to be a beginner again.

Epilogue

We'd be remiss if we ended this book any other way than to allow you an opportunity to add a fifty-first story to it—your story.

Perhaps as you've read through these pages God's Spirit has begun speaking to you, calling you to be a beginner like John Duckworth and his father. Perhaps you feel a yearning in your heart to experience a little of what people like Le Thai, CeCe Winans, James Dobson, Todd Peterson, Hanna Miley, Robin Jones Gunn, Kurt Garland and the others experienced.

Perhaps it's time for you to make your own meeting with God.

The message is simple. All of us—you included—have done wrong. The Bible calls that sin and shows that the penalty of sin is eternal death. That's the bad news.

The good news is that God sent his Son, Jesus Christ, to pay the penalty of sin. Jesus gave his life, suffering and dying by crucifixion, to pay that penalty. Then to show that he was more powerful than sin and death, Jesus rose from the dead, coming back to life with an offer of life to all who would believe. He offers life to you.

Listen to how the Bible describes this:

"For all have sinned; all fall short of God's glorious standard" (Romans 3:23).

"The wages of sin is death, but the free gift of God is eternal life through Christ Jesus our Lord" (Romans 6:23).

"For if you confess with your mouth that Jesus is Lord and believe in your heart that God raised him from the dead, you will be saved. For it is by believing in your heart that you are made right with God, and it is by confessing with your mouth that you are saved. As the Scriptures tell us, 'Anyone who believes in him will not be disappointed' " (Romans 10:9-11).

Now we come back to you. Would you like to experience the salvation that God offers you? If so, it's only a prayer away.

Open your heart to Jesus right now. Pray to him. Ask him to forgive the failings of your past, to erase the penalty of your sin. Ask him to fill you with his Holy Spirit, to enable you to follow him for the rest of your life, to make you a "beginner" in faith. Why not do it now?

After you have prayed, please contact a church near you and let someone know about it. Tell the folks there that you have just given your life to Jesus and would like help to learn more about following him.

And if you think of it, let us know about your personal salvation story too. We'd love to hear from you. You can email us at the following address: nappaland@aol.com.

We look forward to hearing from you soon.

About the Authors

Mike Nappa is founder and president of the Christian media organization Nappaland Communications, Inc. He's a best-selling author with over a half million copies of his books in print. He's been a featured writer in national TV, radio, and print media and is a contributing editor to *CBA Frontline* magazine as well as a columnist for *Living with Teenagers, ParentLife,* and *Christian Single* magazines. His work has also appeared in such Christian publications as *CCM, Crosswalk.com, Christian Parenting Today, Clubhouse, Group, Home Life, New Man,* and *Release.* A former youth pastor, Mike makes his home in Colorado.

Dr. Norm Wakefield is a professor of pastoral ministry at Phoenix Seminary. He is a noted speaker and best-selling author of numerous books, including *Legacy of Joy, You Can Have a Happier Family,* and *Solving Problems before They Become Conflicts.* He also coauthored two books with Josh McDowell, *Friend of the Lonely Heart* and *The Dad Difference.* A former pastor, Dr. Wakefield resides in Arizona.

Index